The
Intrepid
Traveler

The ultimate guide to responsible, ecological,
and personal-growth travel and tourism

Adam Rogers

Third edition

The Intrepid Traveler
Third edition, completely revised and updated
© 2019 Adam Rogers

Phoenix Design Aid A/S
Østergade 19, 8900 Randers C, Denmark

Library of Congress Cataloging in Publication Data
Rogers, Adam, 1963 –
    The Intrepid Traveler
    The ultimate guide to responsible, ecological and
    personal-growth travel and tourism
Adam Rogers, Third edition 2019
Completely revised and updated
ISBN 978-87-999030-9-2

All photos by Adam Rogers except those listed in the appendix.

Design and printing by Phoenix Design Aid A/S, a CO2 neutral company accredited in the fields of quality (ISO 9001), environment (ISO14001) and CSR (DS49001) and approved provider of FSC™ certified products. Printed on FSC certified paper without chlorine and with vegetable-based inks. The printed matter is recyclable.

FSC
www.fsc.org
MIX
Paper from
responsible sources
FSC® C130486

Contents

17: Staying Healthy _____ 291

Ithaka

BY C.P. CAVAFY

As you set out for Ithaka
hope your road is a long one,
full of adventure, full of discovery.
Laistrygonians, Cyclops,
angry Poseidon—don't be afraid of them:
you'll never find things like that on your way
as long as you keep your thoughts raised high,
as long as a rare excitement
stirs your spirit and your body.
Laistrygonians, Cyclops,
wild Poseidon—you won't encounter them
unless you bring them along inside your soul,
unless your soul sets them up in front of you.

Hope your road is a long one.
May there be many summer mornings when,
with what pleasure, what joy,
you enter harbors you're seeing for the first time;
may you stop at Phoenician trading stations
to buy fine things,
mother of pearl and coral, amber and ebony,
sensual perfume of every kind—
as many sensual perfumes as you can;
and may you visit many Egyptian cities
to learn and go on learning from their scholars.

Keep Ithaka always in your mind.
Arriving there is what you're destined for.
But don't hurry the journey at all.
Better if it lasts for years,
so you're old by the time you reach the island,
wealthy with all you've gained on the way,
not expecting Ithaka to make you rich.

Ithaka gave you the marvelous journey.
Without her you wouldn't have set out.
She has nothing left to give you now.

And if you find her poor, Ithaka won't have fooled you.
Wise as you will have become, so full of experience,
you'll have understood by then what these Ithakas mean.

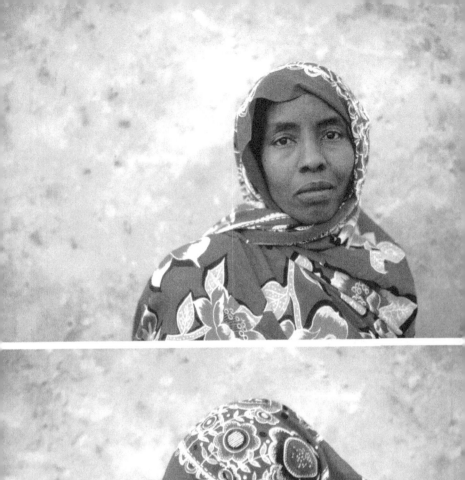

The second dimension of intrepid traveling involves getting to know the people and their culture, gaining a glimpse of empathy into how life is experienced through their eyes.

Preface

> "The use of traveling is to regulate imagination by reality, and instead of thinking how things may be, to see them as they are."
>
> – Samuel Johnson

The Greek poet, Constantine Cavafy, wrote in the late nineteenth century of the importance of enjoying the trip, any trip, and not only longing for a journey's end. It's a metaphor that can be extended to many of life's processes and what this book is ultimately about.

This book is about travel – not tourism per se, but travel – experiential travel; the kind of travel that benefits both the visitor and the visited. And not just the travel where you go for a good time – though if you follow the guidance in this book carefully, I do believe you will have the time of your life, far beyond what you ever thought possible.

In the history of this world there has never been a better time to explore and never a greater need for increased awareness of the principles and practices of responsible, ethical, sustainable, and experiential travel. This is what I like to call intrepid travel, as the word intrepid suggests a lack of fear in dealing with something new or unknown – indeed seeking out the new and unknown to better understand the world as well as oneself. The adjective comes from Latin *intrepidus*, formed from the prefix in (or "not") plus trepidus ("alarmed"). In other words, a traveler who is not alarmed: an intrepid traveler.

Intrepid travelers are among a group of daring individuals who want—indeed thirst—for a deeper understanding of the world in which we live. To travel is to step beyond the comfortable surroundings of the familiar world. I believe this is one of the greatest adventures we can take in life.

Whether you are planning a trip to Argentina, Bangladesh, China, Denmark, Ethiopia, France, or Germany (or Haiti, India, Jamaica, Korea, or Lichtenstein), traveling offers an opportunity for the ultimate adventure and the highest education, if you are open to it. To travel is to live life at its fullest.

I believe that travel is best when one pursues a three-dimensional experience, with three separate but interlinked facets of reality. There are the things we can see with our eyes—images captured on postcards, the monuments left behind by past civilizations, the architectural remnants of yesteryear. And then there are the people—the descendants of those who built the pyramids, the Great Wall of China, or the temples of Machu Picchu. The second dimension of intrepid traveling involves getting to know these people and their culture, gaining a glimpse of empathy into how life is experienced through their eyes. The third dimension involves nature—tuning into the vibration of the land and listening to it with all five senses.

This book is part travelogue, part travel guide—to anywhere. The insights that I share in these pages took years to develop, and I am still working on them. My first real travel experience occurred at the age of ten, when my parents packed up the Chevy Suburban, loaded me and my two sisters into the back, and then set off from the south of Arizona to the Yukon Territory in the far north of Canada. I wasn't sure where we were going or why were we leaving, or even what Canada was, although I distinctly remember two words that often came up in the conversations emanating from the front seat: Nixon and Vietnam.

My next big travel experience came at the age of sixteen, when I hitchhiked from the Yukon, down the Alaska Highway to Los Angeles and then back by way of Wyoming and a short stint at the National Outdoor Leadership School. The following year, I bought a used motorcycle and spent a summer exploring the Pacific Coast of North America from Haines, Alaska to Cabo San Lucas, Mexico – reading *Zen and the Art of Motorcycle Maintenance* by the light of campfires along the way. By the age of eighteen I had run out of exciting places to explore on my own home continent and so I set my sights further East—so far East that my goal was to arrive back in the West. This journey took me around the world, lasting five years and through fifty countries throughout Africa, Europe, the Middle East, and Asia on a shoestring budget of less than one hundred dollars per month.

During those five years, I practically lived five lifetimes. Each country, town, and village touched me in some way. Every person I encountered enriched me with a new understanding of life. It is often said that seeing new outer horizons broadens one's inner horizons, and indeed for me, traveling caused my worlds to expand far beyond what I thought possible at the time. Not a single day passed in the five years I spent on the road that my awareness did not expand through a new insight or revelation.

A word about past editions of this book

The first and second editions of this book were not necessarily written for the jet setter. I started out with the backpacker in mind, like myself many years ago. I have since learned that the jet setter, the business traveler, or humanitarian worker can all be experiential travelers, intrepid travelers; responsible adventurers with an appetite to partake of the banquet of life, traveling to explore and experience what is beyond the horizons—the horizons "out there" and those that lie within us.

Indeed, during the twenty-two years I spent working with the United Nations between the second edition of the book and this one, I was able to explore an additional fifty countries in a way that would have been much more difficult had I been an independent traveler on a shoestring budget. From remote rural areas of Mozambique and isolate villages of Cambodia to the deserts of the Sahara and the mountains of Nepal, I was tasked with connecting with, interviewing, and photographing villagers and local authorities throughout the Least Developed Countries (LDCs). LDCs are a group of forty-seven developing countries that, according to the United Nations, exhibit the lowest indicators of socioeconomic development. Some of the images and insights in this edition are from those experiences.

Whether your budget is one hundred dollars per month or $1,000 per day, the two things I believe you must bring with you as an Intrepid Traveler are an open mind and curiosity. You can be eighteen or eighty years old and travel with a backpack, a duffel bag, or a suitcase. You can wear jeans or a suit. The externalities are secondary. A wise monk in a monastery in Thailand once told me that it is the motivation behind the action that determines the quality of the experience. It is precisely your motivation to travel that will be the greatest determining factor behind both the quality of your experience and whether it builds you up or breaks you down.

There are as many reasons to travel as there are travelers themselves, but there is something that ties even the most diverse of travelers together: a sense of adventure, a heightened self-confidence, and a positive outlook on life. Travelers are characters that seldom sit still. They are always wondering what is on the other side of the mountain. The tourist tours, usually in groups, and he focuses most of his attention on seeing, on "window shopping." Travelers are usually highly motivated, intensely interesting, and wonderfully inquisitive. Their experiences have shown them that the world is indeed a wonderful place. They have a good understanding of global events and feel comfortable with anyone in most any circumstance. She focuses on experience—on meeting people and attempting an empathic understanding of life as viewed through another's paradigm.

It is my vision that through increased travel and a greater understanding of the world in which we live, that the world will become a better place one traveler at a time. Global peace and global stability can only come through global understanding. Understanding comes through connecting and interacting. Connecting and interacting is what you do when you travel.

Every traveler is intrepid—fearless and self-confident. This confidence arises from being able to perceive a goal and achieve it. It also comes from trusting the universe to provide your needs and knowing with confidence that every situation, no matter how complicated or uncomfortable, is an opportunity to learn. We are never presented with a challenge too great to overcome with the right attitude, and every challenge brings with it new understanding and awareness.

It is commonly thought that to see the world one needs a lot of money. The opposite can be true as well; quite often the amount of money spent on a trip is inversely proportional to the depth of the travel experience. In other words, the more money you spend on a trip, the more you may insulate yourself from the people and the reality of the country you are visiting. If you travel to Mexico City, stay at the Four Seasons, eat American food, and travel to all the tourist sites with groups of Americans in air-conditioned tour buses, you may not really be in Mexico City. Rather, you could be merely "seeing" an image through the framed perspective of a tinted glass window. You could probably get better views from watching a documentary on the National Geographic website.

On the other hand, being too frugal carries an opportunity cost, causing you to miss out on potentially valuable travel experiences. I have met travelers who have passed up a visit to a museum or ancient ruins because of a five-dollar entrance fee. If your budget is too tight to allow a visit to a local museum, it may be time to reevaluate your travel plans.

Getting to the part of the world you have planned to visit may the biggest cost you encounter. However, if you plan, compare prices, or make more stops with longer layovers, you can significantly reduce this expense. Once you arrive at your destination, especially if your journey takes you to the developing (and often much more interesting) part of the world, the cost of living and traveling could very well be much less than you expected.

By spending less than the contemporary "tourist," you are more likely to encounter locals and engage them in conversation. By avoiding lunch at the Radisson and instead eating in a local restaurant, by avoiding the tourist bus and instead taking local transport, and by staying with a local family in a bed-and-breakfast or at an Airbnb, you are more likely to spend time with people who are from the area, which should be one of the three reasons you are there in the first place. The geography and nature may be attractive, the cultural sites and monuments may be interesting, but it is the people you meet while traveling that will make your travel experience one that will enrich your life beyond compare. When you return home from your travels, you will have made new friends with whom you may be in contact for the rest of your life.

Travel slows down time – and we live longer

I have found that in many ways when we travel, and our senses are exposed to new experiences, we pay more attention to the details surrounding us: We become more mindful of the people, the food, the smells, the architecture, etc. Thus, we live more in the here and now because it is in the present moment where we experience reality. When we do this, our perception of time slows down, like when we were children marveling at and learning about the world around us. Remember how long the month before a birthday seemed as a child? Then, as we get older, we fall into routines and an entire year can go by in the blink of an eye.

I believe we are only truly alive when our consciousness is anchored in the here and now. When our mind is mired in memories of the distant past, we get lost in movies of our own making. We are not *here, now*. When we are anticipating or worried about events that may or may not happen tomorrow, we are not *here, now* – we are literally somewhere else in our minds. We are only alive, when we are *here, now*, in this moment. Thus, the secret to longevity could be as simple as staying present and mindful in the present. Ponce de Leon's Fountain of Youth as it turns out, is not in some hidden faraway Floridian fable—it is right here where I am, in this moment. It is in observing and appreciating the details of my now.

Inward/outward simultaneous travel

While you are on your outward global journey to faraway lands, you may discover another journey occurring simultaneously. You will see, hear, smell, taste, and feel things that will stimulate your spirit and awaken your senses. These new senses will inspire you to contemplate different paradigms about life and how it is lived. Traveling can transform nearly anyone into a philosopher and poet, for life on the road is revealed to you in a wonderful tapestry of contradictions and the kind of raw beauty that defies definition.

Seeing the world as it is in its true nature is what gives the traveler a perspective of life that is often different from those who have never traveled. The journeyer is more apt to view him or herself as a citizen of the world, of the human race, rather than citizen of a country or representative of a specific race.

I have found that for me, traveling quite often awakens a primordial nomadic instinct that creates a desire to forever want to see and experience what is beyond the next horizon. The more we experience, the more we want to experience.

For those who have never tried it, the traveler's wanderlust can be a curious and rather incomprehensible type of behavior. Some non-travelers even look upon the traveler with either contempt or detached awe, saying to themselves, "I wish I could do that if only _____."

If you want to travel, there is no excuse to delay. Settle your accounts, pay your bills, take an indefinite leave of absence from work, and hang a sign on the window that says, "Gone fishing – in Tasmania."

A few notes on the third edition and some acknowledgements

Twenty-five years in the making, I do hope this third edition of *The Intrepid Traveler* will be of use and interest to travelers who are embarking on their first journey and to those seasoned travelers who can ever-so-well relate to the autobiographical experiences I have included to illustrate a few of my points. I also have tried to write it in such a way that it would appeal to readers who are embarking on the journey of life without transporting their physical bodies to the far reaches of the planet. Armchair travelers can be intrepid as well, gaining every bit as much insights to feed their curiosities and open minds.

This third edition includes a lot of material that simply did not exist when I was doing and living the research for the first two editions. In the early 1980s when I first set out to discover the world there was no email, no internet, and no ATM machines. Placing an international phone call could take three days if there was even a phone available. A letter could take three months to reach its destination. Now all that is required to let mom know you are safe is a Facebook account and access to an internet café or a smartphone.

Also, in the twenty-five years since the first edition of this book was published, I have more than doubled the number of countries I have visited—many during the past two decades of work with the United Nations. I have expanded the sections on traveling as a couple, having experienced much of the world from Marrakesh to Manhattan and from Cairo to Cape Town with my patient and loving wife, Gillian. I also have experienced the joy and adventure of traveling with children and have journeyed to and through several countries from Egypt to Morocco and from Chile to Canada with my two sons, Sage Mandela and Addison Tafari. Traveling with kids opens new opportunities for experiencing a country in ways I had never imagined.

This is a good place to acknowledge that nothing of substance is ever accomplished without the benevolence, understanding, and assistance of friends, family, and higher powers. In recognition of this, I would like to express appreciation to my mother, Nancy Dryden Lorieau and to my publisher at Earth News, Judy Rae. These two women (and their husbands) gave me the push I needed in the early 1990s to put pen to paper and to produce the first edition of this book. I feel enormous gratitude toward my Grandmother Ruth

Wyatt Dryden and to her son, my uncle Chuck Dryden. I would also like to thank the late Ted Harrison of the Yukon for believing in me, Ella Cisneros of the Together Foundation for inspiring me, and to Lennie and Alena, for creating a new haven in New Haven. Thanks also to Wes Bernard, who first taught me how to take photos, and to Laura Kullenberg, my first boss in the UN system, who pushed me to take those skills to the next level. Thanks to my lifelong friend, Mark Podhora, for always being there. Thanks to Jim MacIntyre for an open door; Simona Marinescu for an open mind, and Jamrad Saoman for an open heart and for reminding me to breath. Thanks also to Gillian Rogers, Jamie Birdwell-Branson, and Lili Gutierrez for editing the third edition of *The Intrepid Traveler*, and to Dennis Lundø Nielsen of Phoenix Design Aid, for publishing it.

Of the many, many people who helped me out and inspired me along my own journeys around the world: My deep appreciation goes out to Sebastian Copeland (who provided the foreword to this edition), Reinhard Struve of Germany, Salwa el Habib of the Sudan, and the Nazmuddin Family of Eritrea. Thanks to Dimitry Elias Léger, with whom I worked in the post-earthquake rubble of Haiti and who inspired me with his tenacity for writing and the insights of his book, *God Loves Haiti*. I would also like to recognize, with appreciation and gratitude, the Lebanese monk on Mt. Athos, who changed my life one evening with a single conversation about moments and journeys. Lastly, I would like to express my appreciation to Antoine de Saint-Exupéry and the Little Prince, who wrote that "It is only with the heart that one can see rightly; what is essential is invisible to the eye."

This book, as with the two previous editions, is dedicated to the Little Prince in all of us.

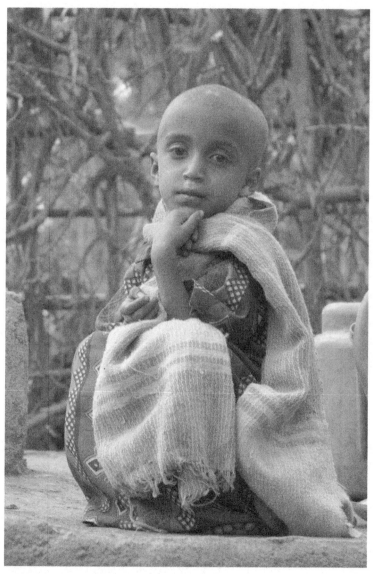

This book is dedicated to the Little Prince in all of us.

Sebastian Copeland is an award-winning photographer, polar explorer, author, lecturer, and environmental activist. He has led numerous expeditions in the polar regions to photograph and film endangered environments.

Foreword

Sebastian Copeland

We live at a remarkable time in human history. Never before have we been able to connect with so many people; to travel almost anywhere on the planet within 24 hours; to hold up our smart phones and see both beauty and destruction. To reach millions of people through social media with the click of a mouse. At the same time, never before has the human race been so perilously close to collapse – and at the same so close to being able to save ourselves, save civilization and finally move together towards a shared and prosperous future, discovering our true inner potential as a people.

Travel and exploration have always been a part of my DNA. I started traveling at a very young age, inspired by my grandfather, who lead safaris across Asia and Africa. He took me on my first photo safari to Swaziland at the age of 12, taking me with him for long walks into the wild. Later on in life I began to explore, on foot, the outer reaches of our planet, from Antarctica to the Arctic.

You need look no further than the Arctic if you want to know what will happen globally in the next 20-30 years. The poles are warming at twice the rate of the rest of the world. Without them tempering the radiation from the sun and the rising heat from the greenhouse effect of the atmosphere, Earth will become less hospitable for humans and most of the species with whom we share this remarkable planet.

You don't necessarily need to travel to such extreme locations as I have, but wherever you travel, try and understand and connect with the wonderfully diverse fabric of humanity and the spectacular expanse of what remains of global ecosystems. When you are open to this awareness, you don't even have to travel far – perhaps no further than Central Park if you happen to live in New York City. I do believe the biggest journey we need to take is within, for to travel around the world and to remain the same person as when you left is not to have traveled at all.

When we can resonate with the unique vibration of a specific ecosystem, be it in a rainforest, the desert or on an icefield, we may feel deep within ourselves a profound connection to the Earth and its web of life – beyond an intellectual understanding of the concept to one that resonates within the core of our being. Seeing may be believing but feeling what I am talking about here is to really get it.

I believe that through the kind of responsible, ecological, and personal-growth travel that Adam writes about in this book we cannot help but fall in love with this world, with its nature, and with its many cultures and people. And what we love, we seek to protect and nourish, thus giving hope to global efforts to turn around the many tides of destruction currently threatening our planet and its people.

It's been said a million times: think globally, act locally. I would add to this, travel globally, educate locally – when you are back from your journeys seek to raise awareness of what is happening in the world. Encourage others to travel, but to travel the way Adam writes about in this book – travel that both supports personal growth, and in some small way contributes to the places visited, and to making this world a better place in which to live, for everyone.

1:

Raison d'être

"The traveler sees what he sees.
The tourist sees what he has come to see."
— *G.K. Chesterton*

Visiting the monumental icons of our human experience on Earth and then shooting selfies in front of them is the primary reason many people travel.

Visiting the monumental icons of our human experience on Earth and then shooting selfies in front of them is the primary reason many people travel—and it is expanding rapidly. According to the Madrid-based United Nations World Tourism Organization (UN-WTO), international tourist arrivals increased from twenty-five million globally in 1950 to 278 million in 1980, and from 674 million in 2000 to a whopping 1.2 billion in 2015.[1]

Cash flows have followed: international tourism receipts have surged from US$2 billion in 1950 to US$104 billion in 1980, and from US$495 billion in 2000 to US$1.3 trillion in 2015. With currently 1.2 billion tourists crossing borders each year, tourism has a profound and wide-ranging impact on societies, the environment, and economic development.

So, what are all those people going to see?

Many of these travelers are headed off to see the Pyramids, the Eiffel Tower, the Leaning Tower of Pisa, Machu Picchu, Angkor Wat, the Acropolis, Stonehenge, the Great Wall of China, the Taj Mahal, and

---

1   For more information check out the Facts & Figures section at mkt.unwto.org

Easter Island. More people travel from A to B on planes, trains, and automobiles to see things than for any other reason, save for seeing relatives at Thanksgiving or for Chinese New Year.

Perhaps the reason we are so fascinated by such monuments to mankind is that they remind us of our own greatness. Perhaps we seek a sense of immortality in seeing the remnants of past civilizations, like the Great Wall of China, the pyramids of Egypt, or the temples of Angkor Wat.

The angels are in the details

I always recommend visiting the things depicted on postcards in the hotel lobby, but I would suggest slowing down your itinerary and taking your time while you are there to take in the details. In Cusco, for example, while visiting the impressive Cathedral Basilica of the Assumption of the Virgin, take the time to inspect the church's foundation. There you will see the remains of an ancient Inca temple known as Kiswarkancha, with massive stones fit together so tightly archeologists still have no idea how they were moved or put in place. Walk up and down the side streets and you may be amazed at what you find. Look beyond the most obvious and ordinary to find the subtle extraordinary.

While cruise ships are a great way to get to know an interesting group of people, they may not the best way to experience a country beyond the superficial. They can, however, introduce you to a catalog of places to which you can return when you have more time. Visitors from cruise ships are often on tight itineraries and must return to the ship before it sails for the next port. While in port you could meet the most interesting of people and perhaps even fall into a fascinating conversation with a local person that you will not want to end when that whistle blows, and it is time to return to ship.

Three-dimensional experiential travel

As mentioned in the preface, I believe that a place can be experienced through three different lenses. I find it best to divide as much time as possible into the following three experiential dimensions to get the ultimate experience from a journey. The three experiential dimensions are as follows: 1) the people of a country and their culture, 2) the monuments to greatness which they have built, and 3) sensing the ecosystem's natural rhythm, be it on the beach, in the desert, or in the forest.

In Egypt, for example, spend time at the pyramids. Visit the people and listen to their stories and then travel into the desert or sit on the banks of the Nile. Listen to the sound of the wind as it blows across the Sahara, rustling palm leaves high overhead, and the gurgling of the Nile as it carries water out of Ethiopia and Uganda on its way to the Mediterranean.

American author Gail Rubin Bereny once commented that the most important thing anyone can bring on a trip abroad is an open mind. You can forget your toothbrush, your camera, or even your underwear, but don't forget an open mind. You will be exposed to many different philosophies and ways of doing things and some of these may seem bizarre and even "wrong." But it is important to remember that you are there to learn, not to judge.

This does not mean that you must accept everything blindly. On the contrary, there is a lot of injustice in the world and you are bound to come across some of it. But question the value of voicing such judgments. You are bound to make certain character assessments of people as will be discussed in the chapter on avoiding trouble. The issue here is to draw a fine line between discerning and making blanket judgments that may put up a wall between you and the locals. Once that wall is up, you may as well just go home.

Preparation for travel

It is important before leaving to prepare your mind intellectually so that when you get to your destination you will better understand what you are seeing. The best way to do this is to read everything you can get your hands on before you leave. If there is an abundance of information available, it might be best to narrow your selection to those topics that interest you most. If you are going to France, for example, and are interested in culinary delights of antiquity, you can go to your local library and look up everything under French food and history. YouTube is another great place to get information on your intended travel destination, both for professionally shot documentaries and home movies. I would also recommend local music videos. (If you're going to Turkey you may enjoy the music video, Mr. Toot, by Ylvis, on the tensions between modern and traditional music).

Do enough research so that you will know what to seek out when you arrive but keep enough time in your itinerary for the unexpected delights you did not read about. You will hear about many places and experiences from fellow travelers and locals once you arrive.

Knowing about the history of a place—both distant and recent history—will give you a sense of perspective and meaning, but it will also warm the hearts of the locals, allowing them to see you as someone who cares and not someone there just to hang out on the beach or in the bars. In 2010, while organizing a UN summit of cities in Dublin, I found my working relationship with local colleagues greatly improved when I read a book on the history of the city and knew something about the many Irish monuments and street names, connecting them with important families in the city's history.

I never had much of an interest in history until I started traveling. While visiting ancient ruins in France, Turkey, and Syria, I found it fascinating to read about the history of the Roman Empire. While climbing the steep trails of the Camino Inca in the Andes, I became fascinated with pre-Columbian history of the Inca. To understand the way things are, it is helpful to know about the events that created the present. If you go to Pamplona to run with the bulls, read up on Spanish—and especially Basque history—so that you can understand both why they are running with the bulls and how the Basque differ so greatly from the Spanish.

Knowledge of politics is also important to get an idea of what is happening around you and to be able to talk to the people you meet about the issues that affect them most. To familiarize yourself with the politics of the region you plan to visit, go online and read newspaper stories on issues surrounding the area. *The Economist* intelligence unit reports are very useful in encapsulating the political reality in every country on Earth in a few pages. English newspapers—in hard copy and on your iPad—are available nearly everywhere, especially in former British colonies like India, Sri Lanka, Malaysia, and Kenya. These papers can be a reliable source of news about the political situation, even if you must read between the lines.

Read about the ethnology and culture of the places you intend to visit, and you will have a deeper understanding of the people you meet. When going to India, for example, read about the Aryan invasion of the sixteenth century B.C. and both the Dravidian and Harappa Valley civilizations. From this you will understand how the people of Northern India are related to the Aryan peoples of Europe and Iran and you will not be surprised or alarmed when you see Swastikas on sacred Hindu temples. You will know that the Swastika is a sacred and auspicious symbol in Hinduism, Buddhism, and Jainism and dates back at least 11,000 years before a certain German leader transformed it into a symbol for tyranny and racial superiority.

After familiarizing yourself with the politics, history, and cultures of the region you plan to visit, the next thing you will need to learn is what to visit in the country and where to go. Books like the *Insight Guides* make excellent preparatory reading. Others, such as the Lonely Planet and Let's Go guidebooks, are always good to bring with you, but are also worth reading before you go. These days you can simply download them on a tablet and carry that with you.

Although there is a lot of knowledge available online, try writing the cultural attachés of the embassies or the tourist offices of the countries you plan to visit and request information. You could send an email but try writing a letter the old-fashioned way and see what happens. Tell them in the letter that you are a student and would like to visit their country to help you in your studies. Most of the material they send will probably be tourist literature, but you may find some of it informative. I've had embassies send tapes of their traditional music, posters of cultural and scenic sites in their country, and books on everything from history to religion.

Find out if anyone you know has been to your destination or knows of someone who has. Read the blogs on tripadvisor.com and digitalnomadtravelmag.com and reach out to the people who have left written accounts. This kind of first-hand travel advice will be your greatest source of information on the road as you meet people coming from places you plan to visit next.

Culture shock and burn out

You've done it. You've taken the step. You boarded the flight and are now in a country far away from the one in which you are accustomed. Your senses are encountering new and exotic experiences. You start to feel alone, isolated—a stranger in a strange land.

In our normal environment, much of our behavior, like gestures, tone of voice, how we line up for tickets, or how we interact with others relies on collectively understood cultural cues. Often, we take all these for granted because they're our unspoken norms; we become more aware of these cultural subtleties when we first travel abroad because they are different from our own.

Step back, take a deep breath, and look around you. It is not at all uncommon to experience what is known as culture shock, or the inability to relate to your surroundings. Culture shock is nothing more than your senses beginning to wake up. Your senses have been used to the same routine for so long, and now can stretch their resilience, stimulated by the new and exotic. *However*, there may be a problem adjusting to the new environment and that is where you need to consciously step in.

Scientists and doctors have for years tried unsuccessfully to define culture shock. While it is difficult to define, it is possible to see the events that contribute to it.

As a foreigner, you will find that you stand out, often like a sore thumb. The reactions other people have toward you will affect you after a while. You may feel out of place and even feel a sense of rejection. All this is compounded by the fact that you are struggling with the language, endeavoring to figure out the local currency, trying to get used to the food, and so on.

Most people react to culture shock in one of two ways: they completely withdraw from the local environment or they abandon their own culture and take on the new. As with most kinds of illness and shock, the best way to avoid culture shock is through preventative medicine. To avoid the extremes of culture, it is best to be as familiar with the country as you can before you get there. Get as much practical knowledge of the language as possible and learn about the peculiarities of social etiquette.

Let cultural peculiarities be your building blocks to a deeper understanding of the people with whom you are interacting. Ultimately, these blocks will become part of a universal bridge that will bring people of all cultural and religious backgrounds to a place

As a traveler, you will see an enormous contrast in income and living standards among and within countries.

where they can communicate and share insights. By traveling, and merely understanding what is going on around you, you are directly contributing to the creation of a world free of prejudice, hatred, misunderstandings, and conflict.

After a while, I started to realize that by learning about another culture I was somehow learning about myself. The lines between "us" and "them" started to become less defined. All cultures everywhere, no matter how seemingly different, are each in some way an expression of the humanity we all share as one human race, with a single origin and a shared future.

Poverty

During a month in Calcutta, I had a daily ritual of jumping on a bus, riding it for an hour, and then attempting to find my way back to my hotel on foot. On one such day, I met a homeless family on the sidewalk with all their material possessions bundled in sacks. They had a glow of serenity about them that affected me. Not wanting to bother them, I positioned myself about a hundred feet away to watch them.

The grandfather was lying down on a blanket under the shade of a plastic tarp that was strung between a light post and a dead tree. His grandson, who looked to be about five years old, lay beside him, with his head resting on the old man's arm. A woman had tea boiling over a small fire, while her husband prepared small cakes to sell with the tea to people on the street.

The young boy spotted me watching them and he sat up. He said something to his father, who immediately waved me over. I got up and approached them and a small stool was brought. I was served tea and cake. We talked for about an hour, and when it was time to leave, I reached into my pocket for a few rupees to pay for the tea.

"No, we cannot possibly accept any payment for the tea," said the father, obviously taken aback that I would even think of paying. "We invited you. You are our guest."

———

In this book, I often draw reference to travel in the developing world, the under or lesser developed. The new term at the United Nations is "the South," although I must admit this can be very misleading to many people outside UN circles (when I used this term in Washington, DC they thought I was talking about Mississippi or South Carolina). Whatever word we choose to refer to the poor regions of the world, it is where people enjoy fewer privileges than many of us in the so called "developed" world. As a traveler, your journeys will more than likely take you into poor countries since many of the most interesting places to experience are there, and they do make up most of the world—around 80 percent. You may start out in Europe or Japan or Canada, but eventually you will experience the excitement of Egypt, India, Cambodia, and Guatemala.

As a traveler, you will see an enormous contrast in income and living standards among and within countries. Although extreme poverty rates have been cut by more than half since 1990, one in five people in developing regions still live on less than $1.25 a day, and there are millions more who make little more than this daily amount.

There has been significant and measurable progress in reducing poverty in recent decades. According to the United Nations, the world attained the first Millennium Development Goal target, which was to cut the 1990 poverty rate in half by 2015, five years ahead of schedule back in 2010 (according to the United Nations, based on nationally-reported statistics). Rapid economic growth in countries like China and India is largely credited for this goal. However, despite the progress in a few regions, the number of people living in extreme poverty globally remains unacceptably high.

Poverty is more than the lack of income and resources to ensure a sustainable livelihood. Its manifestations include hunger and malnutrition, limited access to education and other basic services, social discrimination and exclusion, as well as the lack of participation in decision-making. Women are more likely to live in poverty than men due to unequal access to paid work, education, and property.

The work to end extreme poverty continues, articulated most recently in what the United Nations now calls the "Sustainable Development Goals" (SDGs), which are a universal call to action to end poverty, protect the planet, and ensure that all people enjoy peace and prosperity by the year 2030.[2] Representing ten percent of world GDP, one in ten jobs and seven percent of global exports, tourism has a decisive role to play in the achievement of the SDGs.

The tourism sector is mentioned in, and must deliver on, three of the seventeen SDGs, namely SDG 8 on "Decent Work and Economic Growth," SDG 12 on "Responsible Consumption and Production," and SDG 14 on "Life below Water." Yet, given the multitude of links it has with other sectors and industries along its vast value chain, it can in fact accelerate progress towards all 17 SDGs. If well managed, the sector can generate quality jobs for durable growth, reduce poverty, and offer incentives for environmental conservation – a triple-win to help countries transition towards more inclusive, resilient economies.

---

2   For more information on the Sustainable Development Goals, please see www.undp.org.

The 17 sustainable development goals (SDGs):

The international community is dedicated to the achievement of these 17 SDGs, but huge challenges remain. Access to good schools, healthcare, electricity, safe water, and other critical services remains elusive for many people, often determined by socioeconomic status, gender, ethnicity, and geography. Moreover, for those who have been able to move out of poverty, progress is often temporary: economic shocks, food insecurity, and climate change threaten to rob them of their hard-won gains and force them back into poverty. It will be critical to find ways to tackle these issues as we make progress toward 2030, the deadline set by the United Nations General Assembly for achieving these goals.

While you are traveling, you may become aware of opportunities where you can use your skills to contribute directly to one or more of these goals. If you have the time, do not hesitate. In fact, doing so may make for the most valuable and memorable part of your trip. As Mother Teresa famously said, we may feel that our contribution is but a drop in the ocean, "but if that drop were not there, I think the ocean would be less by that missing drop."

While most poverty is in developing countries, pockets of it exists even in the more developed, industrialized countries. If you live in any of the big cities from New York to Paris, you will no doubt have been exposed to homelessness and numerous other problems that arise from poverty. In the developing world, however, you will be exposed to severe conditions and dealing with it will take both a prepared state of mind and a compassionate attitude. Some tourists choose to insulate themselves behind the walls of an all-inclusive resort and pretend it doesn't exist. But as an Intrepid Traveler, our mission is to venture beyond the palace walls, to really see the reality of the world and to understand it compassionately, and to contribute what we can (harnessing our own unique comparative advantages) to make the world a better place for everyone, everywhere.

When traveling to a developing country for the first time, prepare yourself by talking to other travelers who have already been there. Look at pictures and try to relate to those depicted. Understand that things are going to be different when you walk off the plane at the other end of your flight. And then once you get to a country, get out and meet the people. You may discover that the poorest of our brethren on this planet can also be amongst the most friendly, soulful, and generous.

A few suggestions on how to help

The United Nations World Tourism Organization (UNWTO) defines sustainable tourism as the following:

> Tourism that takes full account of its current and future economic, social and environmental impacts, addressing the needs of visitors, the industry, the environment and host communities.[3]

In this sense, if you are responsible in your tourism, by visiting a country you are typically directly helping the country financially, and thus helping to alleviate the poverty. In 2015, 29.9 million people spent US$44.5 billion in Thailand, 15.2 million people went to South Africa and spent $8.2 billion, and 10.2 million chose Morocco as their vacation destination, spending $6 billion there.[4]

However, sometimes the money that comes into a country from different kinds of tourism adversely affects the country and should be avoided by the socially-responsible traveler, such as sex tourism or party tourism. In Mexico, much of the money is generated in tourist destinations like Acapulco, Mazatlán, and Cancun where both the environment and the social fabric of the regions have been seriously affected. I believe it is better to spend your money where it has the greatest effect, even if it is only a drop in the bucket.

---

3   http://sdt.unwto.org
4   2015 World Tourism Organization.

According to the UNWTO, to truly benefit the host country sustainable tourism should do the following:

1	Make optimal use of environmental resources that constitute a key element in tourism development, maintaining essential ecological processes, and help to conserve natural heritage and biodiversity.
2	Respect the socio-cultural authenticity of host communities, conserve their built and living cultural heritage and traditional values, and contribute to inter-cultural understanding and tolerance.
3	Ensure viable economic operations, provide socioeconomic benefits to all stakeholders that are fairly distributed (including stable employment and income-earning opportunities and social services to host communities), and contribute to poverty alleviation.

When traveling in developing countries, try to patronize only "locally owned" establishments. Flying to Mexico on American Airlines, staying in an American-owned hotel, and eating food prepared by Americans hardly helps the country you are visiting. The only financial contribution to the country is the bellhop's meager salary or perhaps the tip you left the waiter. Whenever possible, fly on local airlines (some of them, like Thai Airways, are much more comfortable than many American-owned airlines), eat in local restaurants, and ask whether the hotel you are staying at is owned by a local or a foreigner.

Try to help those who are actively working to improve their own condition. Give to street performers, for example, and buy your souvenirs from craftsmen and women in the streets (but please try to avoid buying the body parts of endangered animals, which is illegal). Purchase food from sidewalk stalls and have your shoes shined occasionally. This puts money into the pockets of the people and helps at a grassroots level where it does the most good.

When you return home from a long journey abroad (especially if this was your first extended exploration beyond your horizons), you may find that you have been profoundly affected by your experiences. Find out which organizations are working in the areas that interest you most and ask them how you can help. Get involved. There are numerous groups working in all areas of development, human rights, famine relief, etc. who need all the help they can get.

Begging

In nearly every country you may visit except Switzerland, you will probably encounter homeless people asking for a handout. But no matter how prepared you think you may be from the beggars in Western cities, who you may find in other parts of the world could shock you if you are not prepared. Begging is a difficult issue with many travelers, who are usually economizing every cent to be able to travel. Dealing with begging depends on how you look at it. It is best to have your opinions and ideas formulated before you are exposed to people tugging at your sleeves.

In some cultures, people beg because they have no other option. In India, for example, the outcasts usually cannot find employment anywhere and must beg to be able to survive. Also, pilgrims in India begs while on pilgrimage, which is for most of their lives. Giving to these people is considered a way of life, and the locals believe that refusing to give may generate bad karma.

In most parts of the developing world, there is not the kind of government assistance programs that helps the crippled and

Purchase food from sidewalk stalls and have your shoes shined occasionally. This puts money into the pockets of the people and helps at a grassroots level where it does the most good.

underprivileged like in some countries of the West. Thus, people in these countries who are too old, too weak, or physically unable to work often have no choice but to beg for a living.

While traveling, you cannot give to everyone who asks, or you will not have any more resources to continue traveling. Who to give to and when to give is a hard call to make. I find that trusting my gut-level instinct is best. When something inside says this person needs a break, I reach into my pocket and let my intuition dictate how much. I usually give to street musicians, buy local handicrafts, and purchase refreshments in the street from local vendors.

Keep it right

In most of Africa, the Middle East and Asia, the left hand is considered unclean, and thus should never be used to give something to another person, such as when paying for something. Likewise, when giving to a beggar, never pass over your money with the left hand. Though he will probably still accept the gift, he will most likely be insulted. Hand it to him with the right hand and with your left hand on your right forearm. This way, you give the person both money and respect. When you do this, the recipient will probably accept the money in the same manner, taking it up to his forehead and then blessing you with a benediction.

There are times when you should think twice about giving. I have heard that some mothers in some countries cripple their children, so people will feel sorry for them and give more money. If you see a child who is crippled in such a way that it may have happened on purpose and your heart moves to want to help, buy some food for the child and watch him or her eat it.

2:

Soulful Travel

"We always know which is the best road
to follow, but we follow the road that we
have become accustomed to."

— *Paulo Coelho*

Whatever your early motivation to begin the journey, I believe that nearly all travel leads, sooner or later, to an awakening of the soul.

I had been hiking along the Annapurna trail in the Himalaya for about ten days when the path began to climb precipitously into the clouds. I was feeling very proud of myself and confident in my step as I'd prepared for every eventuality by renting the best possible equipment in Pokhara, which is a provincial capital in Eastern Nepal. My pack weighed at least 40 kilograms and my boots were of the rugged variety I often wore as a prospector exploring for gold on the Yukon/Alaska border. I felt like Sir Edmond Hillary, Tenzing Norgay, and Neil Armstrong all rolled up into one rugged climber fueled by his superior testosterone as he sought to circumambulate the great Mount Annapurna in the heart of the Himalaya.

"Excuse me sir, may I pass?"

I looked around and saw behind me a thin, energetic, smiling Hindu pilgrim on his way to the Temples of Muktinath, where worshipers of the god Shiva gather around a spot where natural gas emits a constant blue flame from a crack in the rocks. He wore plastic slippers on bare feet, a sarong tied around his waist, and a thin, worn sweater that looked like it had not been washed since it was made. He had wrapped up all his earthly possessions in a ball the size of his head, which he tied to the end of a stick that rested on his shoulder.

As I stepped aside to let him pass he put his hand on my shoulder and told me, "You will never get to where you need to be carrying all that baggage."

Suddenly my pack seemed much heavier, but I trekked on, reaching Muktinath a day later.

—

Whatever your early motivation to begin the journey, I believe that nearly all travel leads, sooner or later, to an awakening of the soul. It may not start out that way, and many may not even be aware of this transformation until years later, but it is there. While in some way soulful travel is infused between the lines of every chapter of this book, this chapter is oriented toward the primary or central reason for travel being part of an effort to dig deeper into the meaning of life and purpose.

Learning about and from the religions of the world

Among those who may adhere to one religion or another, the topic of religion sometimes inspires an "us versus them" response, with one side of course walking the true path while the others are, at best, deserving of pity and at worse misguided infidels, condemned *ad infinitum* for missing the boat to eternal salvation.

Efforts to reach beyond the beyond to seek a deeper understanding of "what it is all about" is at the core of most people's *raison d'etre* and makes up so much of the core substance of culture. To sidestep it, or worse, discount it as irrelevant, would be to miss an opportunity to connect with the people of a country and perhaps even an opportunity to connect with yourself.

I know I may be stepping out on a limb here with some readers but please bear with me. I would like here to explore the "soulful" dimension of travel, as viewed from my own experience and point of view. When reading, keep an open mind and be aware that the words we use are limiting and limited in scope, especially when we speak about religion or spirituality. Even those two words are not necessarily mutually exclusive but can raise strong opinions from people who have particular associations with them.

Religion as the destroyer and as the preserver

I should reveal at the outset that I am weary of giving or taking any personal guidance or advice about religion or spirituality for I do believe it is about our own personal journey—be it on an established path or one of your own making—that will ultimately bring you to your own destination that is of the most value *to you*. I also believe that the degree of exuberance infused in one's passion for evangelism is often inversely proportional to the depth of one's own spiritual insight. In other words, oftentimes the ego may feel a need to convince others to maintain confidence in the dogma that has been embraced. "If I can convince someone else that I am right, then I *must* be right…"

I have seen how religion can demolish societies, but I have also witnessed how religious insight and inspiration can illuminate people in ways that enable and empower them to reach deep within and realize their fullest potential as human beings, doing an enormous amount of good in the world. I have often pondered how such a powerful force can be both the destroyer and the preserver of life and have concluded that when religion is only in the head it can be the most destructive force on earth, while when it is centered in the heart it can bring positive transformational change within and without.

I do not believe the inspiring sources of each religion (Buddha, Jesus, Mohammed…) intended for those they inspired to memorize the full texts of their teaching, as "the word of God" and then to interpret and defend each letter as if it were sacrosanct. I believe that when you read them carefully, each of the great books from the Upanishads to the Bible reveal themselves as guidebooks full of metaphorical signposts, each meant to nudge the reader in a certain direction where he or she might be able to experience directly whatever it is that inspired all the writing in the first place. The problem is that we tend to get stuck at the signposts, bowing before them, burning incense and candles, and then arguing about their meanings – not realizing all the signpost may be saying "look within, still your mind, and you will figure it all out yourself."

Religion in the head as opposed to spirituality in the heart

It seems that no matter the religion, if those following it have only the memorized texts in their heads without a deeper awakening within, they will always be at odds with one another and can argue all day and all night with stress, tension, and unease. Furthermore, if there is no one around from another religion or faith to attack, these people will find those within their own faith whom they can start to criticize and transform into "them." Thus, the "structured" forms of these religions keep breaking into smaller and smaller subdivisions, or splinter sects of "us" and "them."

However, I have met religious people in all corners of the globe and of every faith, Muslim, Christian, Jewish, Buddhist, Hindu, etc. who all seem to "get it" and can harmonize with one another, anchored in their hearts, but exploring with their minds. There is always a peaceful harmony when around these groups. They realize there is no "us and them"; there is only "us," which is currently seven billion of us on a warm rock spinning through cold space trying to figure it all out.

Thus, I have come to believe that if our religious or soulful pursuit is anchored in the mind/brain, the heart seems out of reach in most cases. Yet if we seek to orient ourselves from within the heart, the soul, or whatever one calls this depth of unknowing within, then we will come closer to experiencing what it is that inspired the formation of these religions in the first place. Responding to a question from the Pharisees about when the Kingdom of God would come, Jesus said, "The kingdom of God does not come with observation; nor will they say, 'See here!' or 'See there!' For indeed, the kingdom of God is within you."

No matter the religion, if those following it have only the memorized texts in their heads without a deeper awakening within, they will always be at odds with one another.

Parliament of world's religions

Over the past 125 years there have been several global conferences referred to as a Parliament of the World's Religions, with the first being the World's Parliament of Religions of 1893, which was an attempt to create a global dialogue of faiths. For a hundred years, the faiths chose not to dialogue, but the centenary of the first meeting led to a new series of conferences under the official title: Parliament of the World's Religions.

A few years before she became my wife, Gillian and I traveled to Cape Town, South Africa in December 1999 to attend the third Parliament of the World's Religions. We traveled there together with the very reverend James Parks Morton, a retired Episcopal priest and founder of the Interfaith Center of New York, and Isaac Tigrett, founder of both Planet Hollywood and the House of Blues. Isaac wanted to create a third chain of restaurants called The Spirit Channel that would also have a virtual space on the internet. While Planet Hollywood celebrates the achievements of the silver screen and the Hard Rock Café showcases hard rock, Isaac's vision for The Spirit Channel was to celebrate the world's faiths in a way that one could learn from and appreciate each for its contributions to the story of humanity.

The Cape Town conference began with a speech from Nelson Mandela, who acknowledged how religion has provided the basis and has even given legitimization to violent expressions of intolerance and conflict. We were so impressed by Mandela that we decided to name our first son after him.

"Few other dimensions of human life reach such a massive following as the religious," said Mandela in a speech transcribed by Gillian for The Spirit Channel, "Its roots are in every nook and cranny of society where political leaders and the economically powerful have no sway."

My point here is that as a traveler through life, we would miss out on much that life has to offer if we discount religion—in all its forms and expressions. Each religion has something to teach us, both in our mental preparation for travel, but also perhaps for the heart, soul, or inner being that is somehow separate from our cerebral centrism.

As a traveler exploring life beyond borders, to miss out on how the people of that country find meaning and purpose would be to miss out on much of what that country is about. If you're in the Middle East, study the Abrahamic faiths, visit a mosque, or talk to the people worshiping there. In Asia, do a Vipassana retreat. In India, hang out in an ashram. If visiting the United States, find a way to attend a sweat lodge ceremony with Native Americans (or First Nations in Canada).

Blood brothers?

When I was nineteen years old and not long after walking from Jerusalem to Bethlehem with a group of pilgrims on Christmas Eve, someone approached me to donate blood at a Palestinian hospital. Someone had been shot and needed blood. After that (a few days later), to even it out, I also donated blood at a Jewish hospital.

This led me to an idea that I then had blood brothers (or sisters) on both sides of the Israeli/Palestinian conflict. Henceforth while on my round-the-world journey over the next five years I donated blood in nearly every country I visited, with the idea that somehow, I would have blood brothers around the world of every possible ethnicity. I am not sure of what relevance this anecdote has in a

Soulful travel is to travel with an open mind, learning from all paths and teachings along the way.

chapter on soulful travel, except to say that this was my own way of recognizing and supporting my family of humanity.

We get so caught up in separating ourselves from others by such superficial externalities as skin color, body size, and gender that we fail to see them as who they really are inside and beyond the superficial externalities of their shell. For my own personal journey, the simple act of donating blood started a process of inquiry that eventually led to my own realization that my body is but a vehicle that my soul has chosen to get from A to B in this time and space continuum called life.

From my own view, I see people focusing too much on their "vehicles" that they somehow miss out seeing the person driving. Their upbringing, education, and societal conditioning has taught them to value a certain type of car over others—perhaps a Lamborghini or Mercedes—and with a preference for a color and body type. They seek to be near those "vehicles" and to admire and appreciate them—perhaps even marry one—only to discover many years later there is a person inside that car, driving. Often, we put so many layers on top of each other—skin color, body type, clothes, salary, and the house we live in—that may or may not say anything about the person underneath it all.

I am not saying not to appreciate the things of this world. On the contrary, one of the reasons I have come to believe there is a world is to both appreciate and learn from all the experiences that it has to offer. But when we attach ourselves to things, this path can lead to separating us from one another and from ourselves. In other words, we start to see ourselves as the skin we wear or as the things we have. We lose sight of ourselves and of others.

Pilgrimages

The difference between soulful travel and a pilgrimage could be that a pilgrimage involves a preordained destination like Mecca or Santiago de Compostela on the Camino de Santiago. Soulful travel in my view is to travel with an open mind and an open spirit, learning from all paths and pilgrimages along the way. However, one can combine the two, setting off on a pilgrimage. But instead of focusing too much on the destination, focus on each step of the way.

In my own personal journeys, I have often combined pilgrimages with other forms of travel. For example, after traveling for six months around Europe at the age of nineteen, I headed to the ancient monastic state of Athos to learn about the Christian Orthodox faith.

Mount Athos is both a mountain peninsula in northeastern Greece and an important center of Eastern Orthodox monasticism. It has been inhabited since ancient times and is known for its nearly 1,800-year continuous Christian presence and its long historical monastic traditions. Today, more than 2,000 men from Greece and many other countries, including Eastern Orthodox countries such as Romania, Moldova, Georgia, Bulgaria, Serbia, and Russia, live an ascetic life in Athos, isolated from the rest of the world. It is governed as an autonomous polity within the Greek Republic under the official name Autonomous Monastic State of the Holy Mountain. If you are a man (women and female creatures of any kind are strictly forbidden), in search of both adventure and growth in the spiritual realm, this may be your perfect destination. It changed my life, as I am sure it would change yours. However, keep in mind that each pilgrim will come away with a different experience of what is Mount Athos, and each one will be perfect.

After explaining to a monk from Lebanon, who had been living on Mount Athos for quite some time, that I was fulfilling a dream to travel around the world on a shoestring budget by venturing evermore eastward until I arrived back in the West, he told me:

"When you are embarking on your path around the world discovering all that which you can see with your eyes, be sure not to neglect the path your soul is taking simultaneously in a world that you can discover only with your heart."

And thus, I began my own personal, soulful journey.

Seeing a head in Syria
From Mount Athos, I traveled from Greece, overland through Turkey and found myself in an unexpected pilgrimage into Islam in Syria with a Mullah of the Umayyad Mosque, also known as the Great Mosque of Damascus. Located in the old city of the Syrian capital,

the Umayyad Mosque is one of the largest and oldest mosques in the world and is considered by some Muslims to be the fourth-holiest place in Islam.

I was at the mosque with the rather morbid motivation of seeing the head of John the Baptist. Those readers who are familiar with the Christian Bible will remember that King Herod of Galilee (under the Roman Empire) had imprisoned John the Baptist because he reproved Herod for divorcing his wife and unlawfully taking Herodias, the wife of his brother Herod Philip I. On Herod's birthday, Herodias' daughter Salome danced for the king with such grace that Herod promised to give her anything she desired, up to half of his kingdom. When Salome asked her mother what she should request, her Mom asked for the head of John the Baptist on a platter. Although Herod was appalled by the request, he reluctantly agreed and had John executed in the prison. His head has remained encased in a shrine to this day and is presently at the Umayyad Mosque in Damascus.

In an unexpected turn of events, while admiring John's head, I was approached by an Islamic priest, who invited me to stay at the mosque with him and to learn the prayers of Islam. I accepted and, in the process, gained an insight into a religious faith that has influenced much of the world for the past fifteen centuries—and me for the past thirty-five years.

A closer look

The founders of all the world's great religions, in my humble view, came from established and very proud traditions, framed by specific cultural views strongly influenced by their external environment and speaking a language that further defined each individual paradigm.

At a certain point in their lives, each one looked around and asked himself if there could be something more to existence than that in which they were immersed, and that which they could experience with but five senses in a three-dimensional reality. Most retreated into nature, away from familiar distractions, and looked within.

We humans have a certain flare for the dramatic, especially when attempting to convince others that our views are correct. We tend to believe we are awesome or that those whom we adore are adorable. The stories and anecdotes wrapped around the foundational experiences of the great religions may have been embellished somewhat, but one thing of which we can be certain is that

Listen to histories, learn from her stories. Immerse yourself for a while in their stories. But ultimately, your soulful journey will be based on your own story.

most of the founding figures needed to connect with nature, to be alone, and to find something within. Siddhartha Gautama, born in 563 BC, left his cushy palace in Lumbini and ended up sitting under a tree in an area of India known today as Bihar, contemplating the links between causation, clinging, and calamity. Upon gaining an insight and revealing his Four Absolute Truths (to contemplate while walking the Eightfold Path), Siddhartha became Lord Buddha.

Six centuries later, and 5,000 kilometers to the west, legend tells us that Jesus of Nazareth, after being baptized by John the Baptist fasted for forty days and nights in the Judaean Desert, gaining insight into several temptations that distract deeper spiritual inquiry: "lust of eyes" (materialism), "lust of body" (hedonism), and "pride of life" (egoism). Fast forward another 600 years or so and journey 1,200 kilometers southwest and we find the prophet Mohammed alone and in deep prayer in a cave called Hira, located on the mountain called Jabal an-Nour, near Mecca. Per Islamic Insight, the prophet Muhammad was visited in this cave by the archangel Gabriel, who revealed one of the first verses to what later became the Koran.

I mention these three by way of illustration but by no means exclusion. There were many others of whom we know from Bahá'u'lláh to Zoroaster, and no doubt many, many more of which history has not recorded, probably because they were women and history is filled with *histories*—not her stories. My point here is that we can learn from all of them, and from each other, but ultimately the path we seek is not written, but is ours to write because I believe there lies within each of us our own unique connection to the Infinite. Listen to his stories, learn from her stories. Immerse yourself for a while in their stories. But ultimately, I believe your soulful journey will be based on your own story.

3:

Languages

"He that travelleth into a country before
he hath some entrance into the language,
goeth to school, and not to travel."
— *Francis Bacon*

A sign in Iceland reminds motorists to put on their seatbelts. Sometimes a photograph tells a thousand words, without the use of language.

In Zanzibar, after having only studied Swahili for a few weeks at a local language school, I went into the market to buy some milk. Approaching a counter of a small dairy (and eager to practice the phrase I had formulated just minutes earlier) I asked the woman standing there: "Maziwa yako?"

The women then proceeded to grab her rather large breasts with both hands and replied: "Ndio mzungu, ni maziwa yangu!" ("Yes, white man, these are my breasts!")

She and the customer she was talking to burst out in laughter as I realized the mistake I had made. In Swahili, the same word for milk means breasts, depending on how it is used. The possessive pronoun for that particular noun in Swahili is the same as the word for "there is," or "is there." The difference is in the order: Yako maziwa? means, "Is there any milk?" Maziwa yako? means, "Are those your breasts?"

—

While studying French, Spanish, Arabic, and Swahili, all in the countries where they are spoken, I acquired an insatiable appetite for learning languages. I never had a talent nor an interest in learning lingos before traveling, but I discovered there is something wonderfully exciting about communicating with someone in his or her own language and gaining insights into their culture through that language.

Learning a new language can be extremely challenging, especially as an adult, if you're busy and distracted with other priorities and if the language you are trying to learn is based on different sounds than your native tongue.

A second language is always the most difficult to acquire, because your brain needs to get used to associating new sounds with the world around you, and then memorizing them in different parts of your brain so they don't confuse one another. If you already have a second language, it is usually much easier learning the third, fourth, and fifth languages, because your mind becomes accustomed to filing and separating modes of communication into different compartments in your brain.

Learning another language is a lot of work but has many advantages and rewards that outweigh the time and trouble it takes to learn. Learning a language opens a window into the culture you are visiting, enabling you to perceive and understand cultural subtleties that would otherwise elude you. It opens new avenues for contact and endears you in the eyes of your hosts. Learning a foreign language broadens your horizons of understanding, introducing your mind to different perceptions of the world around you. Studying languages is also a lot of fun, like unraveling a puzzle and putting the pieces together as you grow in fluency and understanding. Learning another language is also the best way to understand your own culture and language because it causes you to look at your own mode of communication in a more analytical way from an external perspective.

To a certain extent, you need to understand the grammar and structure of a language, but when you start to tear it apart into bilabial this and glottal that, the learning process may not be as enjoyable. Languages are alive—they have a heart and a soul and are constantly growing and changing. To learn a language, you need to be interactive; you need to get out there and mix with the people. I am not saying avoid the books and grammar, but books and grammar reveal the mere structure and rules of a language, not its heart and soul.

English is spoken in more countries than any other language, and by speaking it you have a considerable advantage over people who don't. With English, you can travel to just about anywhere in the world and communicate. This, however, can be a disadvantage, as it gives many English speakers an excuse not to learn other languages. There is a joke in many cultures around the world that a person who speaks three languages is trilingual, a person with two languages is bilingual, and a person who only speaks one language is an Anglo-Saxon.

Don't let this stereotype apply to you. People who don't learn a foreign language because "English is already spoken by most everyone" are missing the point. Languages are not only used for communication; they give you an insight into the culture and an expanded insight on your own worldview. The cultural perspective and outlook on life are manifested in the language.

A word about words

Words are a collection of specific sounds that societies invented and have established agreements. These sounds, when strung together in this way, will represent a certain concept. In other words, the people of England, many centuries ago (before they even reached Britain) somehow put the two syllables together "ah" and "pul" to represent the red fruit that Eve once presented to Adam.

Words have value far beyond the sounds carried on a puff of wind to carry meaning from my brain to yours so that an idea can be transmitted. I believe that how we use our words, and how we respect them, play a very important and critical role in producing positive results for all concerned in any conversation.

Consider carefully that all words carry energy within them based on the way they are said, or not said, and based on their original and intrinsic meanings. For example, in calling someone a "son of a bitch," you are in fact calling their mother a bitch—a very negative thing to say. The word of course has entered common discourse and does not intentionally denigrate a person's mother, but the meaning is still there. Try to find a different word if you are angry with someone.

About 15 years ago, a Japanese researcher by the name of Masaru Emoto revealed the effect of thoughts on the molecular structure of water. Thoughts, when leaked out of the brain as words, take on even more energy so they can carry themselves from voice box and lips at A to eardrum at B.

Emoto's water crystal experiments consisted of exposing water in glasses to different words, pictures, or music, and then freezing and examining the aesthetic properties of the resulting crystals with microscopic photography. Emoto made the claim that water exposed to positive speech and thoughts would result in visually "pleasing" crystals being formed when that water was frozen, and that negative intention would yield "ugly" frozen crystal formations.

One can easily apply Emoto's work to communication. The fact that the human body is made of seventy percent water—through which words and their associated energies can travel so much faster and more effectively than through air—implies that negative words, when directed at a person, can create negative manifestations within that person's body. On the contrary, I truly believe that directing positive words and positive energy can put them on a positive causational trajectory.

The third of eight principles on the Buddha's Noble Eightfold Path is *right speech*. The Eightfold Path consists of eight practices: 1) right view, 2) right resolve, 3) right speech, 4) right conduct, 5) right livelihood, 6) right effort, 7) right mindfulness, and 8) right samadhi (meditative absorption or union, also known as yoga). In other words, paying attention to what you think and say in every language can have positive results in your life.

I do not intend to launch into a treatise on Buddhism here, but if you are interested in taking your travel to the next level, you may want to consider taking a long walk on the eightfold path. In fact, if I could be so bold as to add a ninth dimension to the Buddha's teaching I would suggest *right travel*.

World views defined by languages

By learning another language, we can step inside the culture to see the world as the native speakers do, which is often different from the way the world may be structured by our own language. This phenomenon is known as linguistic determinism and has been studied and explored at length by, among others, Edward Sapir and Benjamin Lee Whorf.

For example, the Swahili word for stranger, "mgeni," is also the word for a guest in one's home. In English, the word for stranger has its origin in strange, as in unknown, unfamiliar, odd, and unusually different. The mere etymological origin of a specific word can influence how we view other people. In East Africa, when one sees a stranger walking by while one is eating, the immediate and habitual response is to invite him or her to eat. In the Anglo-Saxon world we teach our children not to trust "strangers" – presumably because they are "strange" (not like us) and potentially dangerous.

The common Hindi greeting, *Namasté*, means "the highest spiritual quality in me salutes the same in you." It is built within the greeting an acknowledgment that there is something more to life than what we see looking at each other with our eyes. A look at the original meaning of the English word "good bye" reveals "God be with you," or, as in French, "adieu," and Spanish, "adios."

It is interesting that some cultures have no words for conflict. Without a word, there can be no concept unless it is introduced by another culture. Without a concept, there can be no manifestation of the action or thing: It does not exist for that society. By learning the language, not only are you given an insight into a unique way of looking at the world, but when you learn new words, even if they are in another language, your consciousness expands into new realms of understanding of the universe. Understanding other languages enables you to operate in a much larger world than one narrowly defined by unilingualism.

Some people who only speak one language may tend to think their way of seeing the world is the correct one and that any other must be incorrect. Learning another language, and the associated linguistic paradigm of viewing the world, opens your mind up to the possibility that there may be other ways of looking at an event, circumstance, or indeed reality itself. Not that one is correct and the other incorrect—both can be true and correct—like different views of the same mountain, but from different sides. The Matterhorn looks very different when viewed from Switzerland than it does from Italy. Photographs from each side of the border of the same mountain look like very different mountains, yet they are of the same magnificent peak towering over the Alps.

When you return from your travels, having learned another language will help you in your professional life, providing a credential that is as good as another college degree. When a prospective employer looks at your résumé and sees that you can speak one or more other languages, he or she will know that you are flexible, intelligent, outgoing, and insightful. In today's expanding business world, having a foreign language and speaking it well can lead to success.

The suggestions offered in this chapter are only meant to get you started. The rest is up to you. No book, course, or audio series can ever teach you anything. They merely provide you the material with which you teach yourself. Teachers, instructors, books, cassettes, and blackboards are only a medium through which we teach ourselves. Whether you go to Harvard University or the University of Life, you will fail unless you realize that it is only through intent, commitment, and effort that you will ever learn anything.

Learning before you go

The importance of learning as much of the language as possible before leaving home cannot be overemphasized. Every minute you put into building up your foreign vocabulary before you go will enrich your experience immeasurably when you get there. Then once you get there, it will no doubt take off exponentially each day as you interact with the locals.

In an article published in the January 2017 edition of *Scientific American*, Veronique Greenwood claims that listening to a foreign language in the background while you are doing something else can help you learn it faster, even if you are not paying attention. She has concluded, based on research, that exposing your ears to a variety of native speakers just before going to sleep greatly accelerates the language acquisition process.

I love movies and always prefer to watch them in the native language rather than dubbed because an actor acts with his or her voice as much or more than the body. Dubbed-over voices lack the passion of the original acting. If you are studying Cantonese or Mandarin, watch as many films as you can in the original language. If you are studyig a language it helps to watch a film in that language, with the subtitles in the same language. In other words, if you are

Every minute you put into building up your foreign vocabulary before you go will enrich your experience immeasurably when you get there.

studying French, watch French films, with French subtitles. Many DVDs allow this option.

Go to your local community college to see if they offer courses in the language you need to learn. Check listings on websites like Craigslist for local teachers, who are sometimes foreign students eager to make a few bucks and share their language. Most of the major languages should be offered including Spanish, French, German, and Japanese. Most bookstores have CDs on just about every language imaginable, plus books on the grammar. Download some language lessons on iTunes and listen to them in your car on the way to work or school. Start preparing a few months before your departure. Also consider Duolingo, which is a free language-learning platform that includes a website and smartphone app as well as a digital language proficiency assessment exam. The courses are free and fun to follow.

Going to school in the host country

A great way to get an introduction to a foreign country is to first go there to study the language and then set off to explore the country once you acquire the basics. This is especially good if you are going abroad for the first time and feel a bit worried about traveling in an unfamiliar culture. In many programs you can arrange to stay with a family. This is not only a great way to extend your learning beyond the class, but it gives you an insight into the culture, which may have been your motivation for going abroad and learning the language in the first place.

Most universities have information about study abroad programs. Many of these programs are in common destinations in places like Mexico, France, and Spain. See the chapter on *Studying Abroad*, for more information on these initiatives.

It is also possible to do it on your own, which has always been my preference. If you decide to do it this way and need credits to advance toward graduation, you can always take the College Level Examination Program (CLEP) at any college or university in the U.S. or Canada. I studied Spanish for a month in Guatemala and got a year's credit through the CLEP program in Arizona. I traveled to Antigua on my own from Arizona by local buses and boats and found a local school simply by walking around the town. In Tanzania, I found a language school in Zanzibar where I could study Swahili for a year. In Paris, I enrolled in Alliance Française to polish up on my accent and grammar.

Finding your own language school can be much cheaper, more adventurous, and much more effective. You will be on your own and must speak the language. You will not be with people from your university, which is what happens when you enroll from home and go in a group. In fact, if such groups are to be found, avoid them. Hang out with the locals and you will pick up their language more quickly than if you only speak it in the classroom, but retreat to your comfort zone with friends from home afterwards.

Seven billion teachers

The original version of this section in the first edition of the book was titled "five billion teachers." In the past twenty-five years, an additional two billion people have been added to the world's population to help you with your language learning aspirations.

Everyone in the world can be your potential language teacher. With the right approach, everyone loves to explain his or her language to another person—or at the very least to spend a few moments humoring your attempts. Start a large notebook reserved specifically for language and take notes everywhere. If you meet someone on the bus, start an impromptu language class. Not only will it be fun as other people on the bus join in, but it is a good way to meet people. As your knowledge of the language grows, you will meet friends with whom you will only speak in your new language.

Ad hoc theater

A fun way to learn a language, especially if your hosts do not speak a language you know, is to choreograph a theatre. This works well if you are staying with a family. I first did this in Syria, after just having crossed over the border from Turkey. I had to walk most of the way through no-man's land, until I reached an outpost where a local bus could take me to Aleppo. At one of the first villages where the bus stopped to drop off passengers, a young man my age invited me to disembark with him and to have a meal at his house. I ended up staying a week, sharing a meal at the home of nearly everyone in the small community.

On the second evening, we arranged a play so that I could learn simple greetings in Arabic. I would walk outside and then return to the house and knock on the door.

"As-Salaam-Alaikum," I would say, which is the Arabic greeting "Peace be unto you."

"Wa-Alaikum-Salaam" came the response in unison. "And also, upon you."

"Ahlan wasahlan," welcome to our home.

I then greeted everyone, was asked to sit down, and was offered tea. Everyone asked how I was, how work was, and what I was doing. This went on until I ran out of vocabulary, at which time we started all over. This one evening helped me immeasurably and provided a base for learning the language during the next year in the Middle East.

Direct association

The most important thing to know when learning a foreign language, and one that will spell the difference between learning and a botched attempt at learning, is the concept of direct association. When you learn a new word, do not associate it with the English word. Do not, for example, look at an apple that you just bought at the market in Mexico City and say: "An apple...una manzana," and then picture the apple in your mind. Instead, when you learn the word for apple, for example, picture the apple in your mind's eye and associate the sound "manzana" directly to it without going through the English interpretation. Hold an image of an apple in your mind but avoid the word "apple" and go straight to "una manzana."

Direct association may seem difficult at first, but in the long term, it is the easiest and the only effective way to learn another language. Every single day take your new words and picture their concepts in your mind. Write the word, again using your mind's eye, over the picture of the apple, and sound it out repeatedly. Take an apple in your hand, look at it, and say out loud, "manzana." Feel it, taste it, smell it and then eat it, all the while repeating over and over in your mind, "manzana, manzana, manzana. "

This may be harder to do with something like the moon, but picture it in your mind and repeat the new word for it several times ("la luna, la luna, la luna"). The point is to associate the new word directly with the idea. When you do this, you will be surprised how quickly you memorize new words.

Word association

Some language teachers advocate associating the new word with something that sounds similar in English. When you see the object, you want to remember the name of, you will think of the other object and remember the new word.

In my opinion, this only works some of the time and will probably lead to confusion. What you want to do is create a new folder, or a directory, in your mind, into which you file all your new words. When you speak the new language, you want to operate solely from that place in your mind, and not have to keep crossing over to the English folder. Every time you change folders, the flow of conversation is broken. It will seem difficult at first not to switch over to English in your mind, but eventually, as you get enough words and grammar stuffed into your new "mind folder," you will be more confident in that language.

Don't be bashful

Learning another language requires a great deal of humility. You cannot be too proud, or you will never get anywhere with your new language. You cannot be afraid to make stupid mistakes because, rest assured, you are going to make them when learning a language. Just like me and the milk.

Often, the mistakes you make might even be a bit embarrassing. But fear not; your hosts will forgive you because trying to learn their language overshadows any insult you may inadvertently make while fumbling with their language.

Use it or lose it

Use every word you know as much as you can, especially in the early stages of learning a language. This is why I encourage people to learn only practical vocabulary at first. The first thing you should learn when you arrive in a country (after the greetings) is how to count, at least up to one hundred. Then you should learn how to tell the time. With this, practice your new words by approaching people on the street and asking them the time (even if you already know it). Keep doing this throughout the day until it becomes second nature.

Create situations that will require you to use your new words. When you learn the words for different vegetables, go to the market and ask how much each one is. When you learn about directions (straight ahead, left, right, etc.), go out and ask everyone where everything is. When you learn the words for brother and sister, ask your new friends how many of each they have.

What?

If you are Anglophone and want to learn another language, refuse to speak English. If you speak a third language, answer in that language when someone tries to talk to you in English. Tell the person that you only speak Serbo-Croatian, but that you do speak a little of the local language and are trying to learn more. After speaking in the local lingo for a while, you can admit your lie, but only after you have worked on your new language.

If you want to learn the language, you need to decide: I am going to learn this language, no matter what it takes. By taking the plunge and refusing to speak English — no matter how tempted you may be—you will find your knowledge of the language growing beyond your most optimistic expectations.

Teaching your mouth new tricks

Learning a new language often entails learning new sounds. Some of these will seem downright impossible to master and will be the source of utmost humor for your hosts. Do not get frustrated; keep working on them until you get it. Find someone with patience to work with you, and then practice, practice, practice.

Pay attention to what your mouth is doing while making the new sound. Feel what your tongue, lips, and throat are doing when you make normal English sounds. What is the physical difference your mouth makes with the sounds "b" and "p"? Is it a difference of lip movement or air passing through them? How about "r" and "l"? Why do the Japanese have such a hard time with something that to us seems so natural?

Use your smartphone or recording device to get a recording of someone saying the sounds you need to work on. Then retire to your room, and if possible, work on them in front of a mirror.

In French and Spanish, the "r" is the most difficult for English speakers, coming from the throat in French and by rolling the tongue in Spanish. Japanese people have a difficult time with "r" and "l" when speaking English. Arabic has many sounds that come from the middle of the chest and are very difficult to master at first.

Some Asian languages have differences in tone that can completely change the meaning of a word, depending on whether you start high at the beginning of a word and end low, start low and end high, say the word all low, middle, or high. At first, this can seem downright impossible to the Westerner, but with work and patience even this can be mastered. To non-native speakers, the differences at first may sound indistinguishable.

Teaching an old dog some new tricks

It is sometimes said that an old dog cannot be taught new tricks. Having just crossed over the midcentury divide myself, I am starting to wonder if that maxim is true.

Anecdotal meanderings aside, experts now say (well, those experts quoted in a September 2016 edition of the UK publication, *The Guardian*) old dogs can indeed learn new tricks. For much of the history of modern neuroscience, the adult brain was believed to be a fixed structure that, once damaged or overused, could not be repaired or rejuvenated. But research published since the 1960s has challenged this assumption, demonstrating that the brain is a highly dynamic structure, which changes itself in response to new experiences and adapts to injuries—a phenomenon referred to as neuroplasticity. Thus, rest easy: All those old dogs can indeed learn new tricks and should never be intimidated into thinking they can't.

Collectively, this body of research suggests that one can never be too old to learn something new, but with the critical caveat that the older we get, the harder it is for us to do adapt. This is because neuroplasticity generally decreases as a person gets older, meaning the brain becomes less able to change itself in response to experiences. Thus, you can teach an old dog new tricks, but it just takes a bit more patience and perseverance.

Alphabet soup

Quite often, when you are learning a new language, you will be required to learn a new way of representing the sounds on paper. It is doubtful that you are going to be corresponding in the new language anytime soon, especially if it is Arabic or Chinese. But if you are taking a city bus and need to read the destination on the front, a rudimentary knowledge can be very helpful.

Get someone to teach you the alphabet, preferably a child—they have the most fun with that sort of thing. A novice child language teacher would probably be happy to be paid in chocolate. Of course, check with the little one's parents and make sure you are not violating any international child labor laws.

In Chinese, you must learn characters that directly represent concepts, but in most other languages there will be symbols that represent sounds. Write each of these sounds on a small card, and on the back, write several examples of words that begin with that letter. This will not take as long as you might think. Arabic has fewer letters than English, and they usually leave out the vowels, except when writing formally.

Some relatives you can count on

All languages belong to families, and it is easiest to learn a language that is a member of a language group with which you are familiar. For an English speaker, it is much easier to learn German than it is to learn Thai. Hebrew speakers will find many similarities with sister Semitics Arabic and Amharic. Spanish has a lot in common with French and Italian, etc.

Sometimes you will find a connection with a language that has a distant relationship with your own. In India, you will notice that the Hindi word for name is "nom." This is from the Aryan influence of 1600 B.C., which are the same people to which the people of Europe and Iran, belong. In Swahili, the word for table is "mesa," reflecting the Portuguese influence of the fifteenth century when Vasco de Gama swung past the Cape of Good Hope in 1492 and established a small colony in East Africa on his way to India. Conversely, the Swahili word for mean is "kali" – the name of the Hindu goddess of death and doomsday.

If there are any such similarities in the language you are learning, seek them out and memorize them. This will give you a head start.

Find your roots

When studying a language, you will notice words that relate to other words in the same language. This arose out of the evolution of the language when a sound was associated with an idea. When a related idea arose, a derivative of the first sound was applied to it. In English, the simple verb "to relate" gives us related, relation, relationship, relative, relatively, and relativity.

When you sail further into the oceanic vastness of a language you will notice such "relations" between words. Use them. If you have a dictionary in the language you are studying, make lists of relatives and memorize them as part of your daily quota.

Learning ten words a day

A language is made up of words. To learn a language, you must learn sound pattern associations for the concepts you are already familiar with. How many words do you have to learn? That depends on how long you want to stay and how well you want to speak the language. I recommend adopting a pattern of a set number of words a day and sticking to it until you leave the country.

To get around the country and ensure such basic needs as food, water, and shelter, you will only need a few hundred words. To carry on a simple conversation, you will need perhaps a couple thousand. To hold a serious conversation and read a newspaper, you will need at least five thousand. Do not worry about these high figures. Start with just ten words, and then commit yourself to learning ten words a day. If you can memorize more, go for it—the more the better. But be careful, if you try to cram too much in, you will overload your brain and your retention will be hampered.

Some linguists claim that you should only learn seven words a day before overload sets in and retention plummets. I believe everyone needs to find what they can work with; some can learn five, others twenty-five. Just learn as many as you can but stick to a consistent number.

Carry a notebook that is reserved only for language use. Write the date at the top of each page, and make sure every day has your new words on it. After a couple of weeks, you should write both the words and their examples in simple sentences. This will help you to string single concepts into thought patterns. Before long, you will be dreaming in the language.

You do not have to start out your day with the ten words (or whatever number you choose), but just be sure that at the end of the day you can have at least that many on your daily list that you can review before you go to sleep. Carry your notebook with you always and review it when you are waiting for a bus, standing in a line to buy a train ticket, or sitting in a restaurant eating breakfast.

If possible, draw a little picture of what the word means, instead of writing the English translation. This will speed up the learning process. If you are unable to do that, write the English word, but be careful not to cross-associate the two when you are reviewing your list. And when you are out there practicing your new words, try and create situations where you can proudly weave in your new word at least several times that day. If you are learning, for example, the days of the week, try asking a few people what day it is.

The words

When you first get off a plane in a new country and need to start learning the language quickly, there are basic words you should start with. The following is a partial list that you can build on with experience.

» Learn to count from one to one hundred, and from there to one thousand. This is easier than you think because most numbers are repeated in blocks. First, you'll count from one to twenty, then you'll move to words for thirty, forty, fifty, etc., and then you'll move onto words for one hundred and one thousand.
» Practice counting both forwards and backwards. Then, practice instant recognition of numbers on buildings and license plates.
» Learn the pronouns "I," "you," "it," "he," "she," "we," etc., and start to join them with verbs. Learn all the basic verbs and how

they are conjugated such as "to run" ("I run," "he runs," "she runs," "we run," etc.), "to walk," "to buy," "to see," "to say," "to talk," "to want," "to have," "to be," "to travel," etc.

» Learn how to say, "What is this?" and "How do you say _____ in _____?"

» Learn polite phrases. This will help you to become familiar with the language structure. Of particular use are the phrases "please," "thank you," "Where are you from?" "How many brothers and sisters do you have?" and "What kind of work do you do?"

» Learn transitional phrases like "however," "in the meantime," "anyway," and "but." As you grow in proficiency, these phrases can be interjected into the conversation to keep it flowing. Get a small phrase book like those from Berlitz to give you ideas.

» Learn the five Ws: "who," "what," "where," "why," and "when," and then start building sentences with them. (For example: "Who is in charge?," "What is your name?," "What time is it?," "Where is the bathroom?," "Why is it so hot?," and "When does the train leave?") Learn the names of all the objects around you and names of food like "table," "chair," "sky," "tree," "banana," "book," etc.).

» Write down all the common adjectives, including colors you can think of (e.g. "good," "bad," "delicious," "hot," "cold," "close," "far," "big," "small," "pretty," "ugly," "red," "blue," "green," etc.).

The grammar

You can get by in a country through memorizing words, but to ensure retention of the language you will need to understand how the words are put together. If you already have a good understanding of English grammar, learning another grammatical structure will be much easier.

When you study the grammar, you are climbing inside the language. To do this requires a lot of time, tenacious commitment, and hard work. Your hosts will be able to help, but to get the job done you should learn grammar from a book, attend a class for a while, or ideally both.

There are several tenses that should be used in a language to speak it properly. You can always speak in the simple present tense, but if you do this your conversations will always be presently simple. Write down a simple sentence and then learn its different tenses ("I am here," "I was here," "I will be here," "I would be here," "I would have been here," "I have been here," etc.). In some languages, you will discover tenses that do not exist in English.

One of the difficulties in learning languages is that every time you learn the rules of grammar, you must also learn the exceptions. Every language has exceptions to established grammatical rules, but some have more than others. A few languages, such as Spanish and Korean, are very logical. English, on the other hand, is full of exceptions (because it is a polyglot mix of dozens of languages). By learning a foreign language and then realizing how utterly confusing English is, English speakers will acquire a lot of empathy for foreigners attempting to learn English.

Many English speakers have a hard time dealing with the concept of gender in foreign languages. Most languages place a gender relationship on just about every noun and the way it is used in a sentence depends on whether it is masculine, feminine, or neutral. There are a few signs to determine the gender, but there are many exceptions.

In French, if the word ends in "e" there is a good chance it is feminine. If it ends in "o" in Spanish, it might be masculine. One would think that the nature of the noun would determine its gender, but that would be too easy. Both beard and mustache in French are feminine and the word for breasts is masculine.

In Swahili, there are at least seven different concord classes for nouns that are similar to the concept of gender in other languages. Each noun is accompanied by different prefixes on all adjectives and verbs, depending on its class, which also changes in the plural for each one. For example, *kiti kimoja kinatosha* means "one chair is enough," and *viti viwili vinatosha* is "two chairs are enough." Conversely, *kalumu mmoja mnatosa* is "one pen is enough," and *kalumu mbili zinatosha* is "two pens are enough." Sounds confusing, but believe it or not, you do get used to it. And once the structure of the grammar is firmly engraved in your brain, speaking the language becomes a lot easier and stays with you much longer. I stopped speaking Swahili for more than twenty years but then found myself back in East Africa and was shocked when words and sentences starting flowing out of my mouth that I had not used or thought of in all that time.

The best way to familiarize yourself with gender is to pay attention when others are talking, and to the article (the) of the word when you see it written. For example, in Spanish, if it is "el," it is masculine, if it is "la," it is feminine. For years, until I got a better grip on French I would try and make the "le" and "la" sound ambiguous between the two. I felt proud of my innovation, but I am sure my francophone friends were subtly wincing as I castrated their language. Better to get it right the first time and commit the differences to memory.

A few caveats when learning a language

When learning a foreign language, there are a few hurdles and challenges to keep in mind. Telephones, for example, can pose a tremendous challenge when first learning a language and may discourage you if you try to carry on a phone conversation early in your learning process. This is because you can neither see the person's mouth move nor see his or her hand and body expressions. The person on the phone seems to speak unnaturally fast, and the voice is not as clear as it is in person. There is a common belief among communication theorists and academics that fifty-five percent of communication is body language, thirty-eight percent is the tone of voice, and seven percent is the actual words spoken.

When learning a language avoid jokes and swear words. It will be a long time before you understand the subtleties of the language well enough to comprehend a joke, let alone tell one. Most humor does not translate or transfer well from one culture to another. An attempt will most likely be met with benevolent bewilderment. Likewise, swearing or cursing with inappropriate words should be avoided at all costs. You are bound to learn several juicy swear words from many of your impromptu teachers, especially on the street or in bars, but keep them to yourself. These words are good to know but using them will most likely only create uncomfortable situations because they are rarely used with the proper timing and context.

We have all heard foreigners attempting to swear in English, and not using the right word in the right situation and sounding foolish. Swear words carry subtle meanings and are used by fluent speakers at certain times with the right emphasis and intonation. When speaking a language that is not your own, it is better to be safe than sorry.

As you grow in proficiency, you will notice there are times when it is easy, separated by times when you think you are not making any progress at all. The first disappointment usually comes about a month into your experience with the language.

These ups and downs are like foothills separated by valleys, which must be traversed if you are to make the goal you have set for yourself, which is reaching the peak of proficiency in the language. If you are ready for the valleys, you will be able to pick yourself up by the bootstraps and push on.

Learning a language is never easy, but its benefits are boundless. Take the time to learn a foreign language and you will never regret it. There are so many reasons for learning another language today that one wonders why everyone is not out enrolling in foreign language classes. The ability to speak different languages is but another example of the many advantages travelers gain in every aspect of life.

4:

Culture

"Travel is fatal to prejudice, bigotry and narrow-mindedness – all foes to real understanding."
— *Mark Twain*

Once you begin to glimpse life through the lens of another culture, an amazing transformation starts to take place.

Culture is an elusive word. It is difficult to pin down with an accurate description. To some it is theater, to others, the way one dresses. To Webster it is "acquaintance with and taste in fine arts, humanities, and broad aspects of science as distinguished from vocational and technical skills."

For the traveler, culture is found in the people; the way they pursue their needs and interests and the way they express themselves. It is found in the language, the food, the music, and in everyday activities. It is etiquette. It is the way a society perceives life and how a people breathes its values. Culture is what runs through one's arteries, carrying one's *raison d'etre* to the utmost extremes of one's being and then back through the veins to the spiritual heart of existence.

The time spent attempting an empathic understanding of the minute details of another's culture will be in direct proportion to the depth and enjoyment of an overseas experience. Once you begin to glimpse life through the lens of another culture, an amazing transformation starts to take place—rather than the other's culture being something apart from you, it becomes a part of you. Instead of playing into the "us versus them" paradigm—their culture as opposed to my culture—you start to see what hitherto was strange, exotic, and interesting as in some way an undiscovered aspect or a strand of the multifaceted fabric of our own existence. It is *our* culture: A shared, diverse, varied landscape with a myriad of expressions of human existence that are all in some inexplicable way, a part of you.

Eventually you may start to see that there is no "us" and "them." There is only us; currently seven billion of us standing together on a warm rock spinning through cold space, trying to figure things out. When this transformation begins to take place, you may see that anything that appears to divide us—such as the skin color we have or the political borders we live within—as merely illusions obfuscating the realization that we are all One.

Traveling with an open mind and for extended periods of time may enable you to forget about yesterday and where you were; to stop thinking about tomorrow and where you want to go and find yourself instead standing in today, where you are in this moment, marveling at the world around you.

The nomads

Since our species first learned to stand on two feet, we have been on the move—first for survival, then for greed, and then for curiosity. Motivated by these intentions, we have walked to the ends of the earth traversing continents and seas, seeking to get rich through conquering new territories, escaping from those seeking to conquer new territories, or leveraging opportunities to make money from both the conquered and the conquering.

While the politics of global power struggles still sends soldiers to the far ends of the earth, an increasing number of people are traveling across the globe simply to further their understanding of the world in which we live.

Travelers live for the opportunity to see and experience what is out there. In doing so, they have acquired a code of ethics that defines them as a group. Foremost among these is the importance of cultural sensitivity, which cannot be overemphasized as one of the primary qualities of a traveler.

Other qualities that define the traveler are curiosity, a respect for others, objectivity in observation, and the ability to adapt and learn new ways of thinking about the world.

When traveling, all expectations and preconceptions should be left at home. Carrying expectations of the way you think things are or will be creates a filter that deeply affects your ability to experience with clarity what is happening around you. This is because your mind and powers of perception are too busy comparing what is happening with the way you preconceived them to be.

The qualities of a traveler are not necessarily unique to a traveler. For need of definition, I choose the word "tourist" for one who journeys without sensitivity for the culture around him or her and for no further purpose than to have a good time and then brag about being there. A traveler, through his actions, can be a tourist, as a tourist can be a traveler. Traveling can be very beneficial to a country, but tourism—especially sex tourism—is not. Bringing this to light and encouraging "responsible tourism" (i.e. "traveling" can benefit both the visitor and the visited, which is a relationship that has not always been mutually beneficial).

Tourist watching

Quite often, watching tourists in a foreign land can be as interesting as observing the locals. A crowded market place in Chichicastenango, Guatemala offers a good scenario for a study in tourist behavior.

On Saturday evenings each week, hundreds of Mayans descend upon the town from the surrounding mountains. Slowly but meticulously, and with time-worn patience, they build a market on what was hours earlier an empty plaza. The faces of the young and old alike shine with serenity as they work late into the night erecting posts, roofs, shelves, and railings for their goods, with their clothes exhibiting bright, colorful generations of tradition.

An hour before dawn, the plaza becomes a beehive of activity as the vendors and their families put the finishing touches on their stalls. Vegetables of every variety await the nimble touches of a fastidious customer. Flowers and orchids are tied in bunches and laid out in rows of color on the cathedral steps.

In the midst of all this, a few travelers can be seen, moving among the locals and exchanging greetings in Spanish or perhaps an attempt at the local Indian dialect. Their cameras discreetly tucked away, they try to make their appearance as inconspicuous as possible for some of them with blue eyes and blond hair towering two feet above everyone else. But somehow, they do not seem out of place. Their behavior gains the respect of the locals.

At ten o'clock, the tour bus arrives on a day trip from the capital. Huge cameras with 500-millimeter lenses dangle from sunburned necks. Hawaiian shorts and printed t-shirts can be seen pushing through the crowded market, immortalizing moments for the folks back home. Arguments erupt over communication hurdles. Complaints about uncleanliness and bad manners can be heard above the market cacophony.

Respecting local customs

While traveling abroad, you will find that performing normal day-to-day tasks is very different from what you were used to at home.

The more you look, the more things you will see that are different: Things that are almost subliminal in nature, but a very important part of a people's way of life. It can be seen in a handshake, the way one eats, or in simply sitting down.

Personal space, for example, can mean something completely different to an American used to the wide-open range in the Midwest than it does to a Bangladeshi who grew up in a two-bedroom home with sixteen brothers and sisters. People stand much closer to one another in other parts of the world and may stand closer to you than you're used to. Your immediate reaction may be to pull back, but this may be insulting to some people.

These small nuances are very important. Being sensitive to local customs determines the quality of a travel experience. The degree of receptivity on the part of the locals is related to the amount of respect accorded the cultural traditions of the land.

Many customs may seem superficial in nature but can be downright insulting to the local people if not respected. Handing someone money with the left hand, for example, is very disrespectful in most parts of the world, such as the Middle East and India.

Shaking with the left hand or using it to pick up food is likewise unacceptable behavior. Touching someone's head in Thailand is a faux pas of the highest degree and letting the bottom of your foot point toward anyone there (as in Egypt) is like spitting in his face.

It behooves the traveler to train his or her senses to detect slight changes in custom. Of course, reading and asking questions will do much to prepare you, but there will always be subtle unexpected shifts in etiquette that will catch you off guard if you're not ready for them.

All this may seem like an incredible waste of energy to some people, but its value is priceless. It is precisely the observance of culture that weeds out casual tourists from sensitive travelers. Nothing is more obvious than a tourist with complete disregard for local custom.

A perfect example of this is the Westerner who walks around in shorts, impervious to the fact that no one on the street, nor even the entire town, is wearing shorts but him. Unless you are at the beach, wearing shorts in public is disapproved of in many countries. Whether you are in Cairo, Bangkok, or even Tijuana, you will undoubtedly see a Westerner who either doesn't care or is too preoccupied and self-centered to realize what he or she is doing.

The traveler who does not make the effort to respect local culture and etiquette will probably never see the looks of disapproval in the eyes of the people of the host country. The traveler who does will immediately gain respect and appreciation.

The traveler who does not make the effort to respect local culture and etiquette will probably never see the looks of disapproval in the eyes of the people of the host country.

People in many countries have been exposed to a wave of foreigners who care for little more than "having a good time." When they meet travelers with care and concern for their way of life, they open up to them. Once you have touched their hearts, many opportunities will present themselves—opportunities to gain an even deeper understanding of the country you are visiting.

Getting singled out

When traveling in places with strict laws or standards of conduct, at the very least try to avoid behaviors that may draw attention to you. If you blend in, you are far less likely to be singled out. This applies not only to how you speak and behave but also to what you bring with you, such as expensive smartphones, jewelry, and watches.

Cultural ambassadors

Every visitor abroad is a cultural ambassador from his or her country. This means that your behavior can and will shape the opinions of your country in the minds of all those you come across while abroad. The American who gets drunk and obnoxious in a San Francisco bar is just a man who's had a few too many, but that same man in a bar in Jakarta or Munich becomes the "ugly American." Being on one's best behavior is not only considerate from the point of view of your hosts; it leaves a good impression for the next traveler from your country.

There are many American travelers who are ashamed to admit they are from the United States because of the impression the proverbial Ugly Americans have already left. These American travelers are usually the ones to sew Canadian flags on their packs or say they are from another country. This is unfortunate because these Americans are probably the kind of travelers who can set the record straight in the minds of many people in other countries. Americans get a bad rap in many parts of the world, where the typical view of Americans is based on the few tourists who happen by, from their perception of American foreign policy, or from things the United States exports (like *Rambo* movies, Desert Storm, or pornography). Americans will no doubt be challenged to defend their country's reputation, but by being open and honest, foreign citizens will see that there is a difference between a "government" and the individuals from the country.

Women and traveling

While hiking around the Hindu-Kush mountains along the border between Pakistan and Afghanistan, I met Laura, an Irish woman who was traveling alone through the Middle East – overland from Europe to India. A very attractive, red-haired woman in her mid-twenties, Laura said the key to her traveling alone in patriarchal societies was dressing like the local women and respecting local norms and traditions with regards to gender relations. She wore a long dress over a pair of pants and a full shawl covering her hair. She said the men on buses would take special care not to sit too close to her, and always extended courteous respect. She said she felt more comfortable walking the streets of Karachi dressed like a Pakistani than she did in Dublin as an Irish woman.

Women travelers will realize the importance of cultural sensitivity much more quickly than men. Women need to be particularly aware of social norms and accepted forms of behavior for females in the host country, to avoid being hassled by men. The difference between the female traveler who comes back from Egypt with wonderful stories about the people and places she visited and the female tourist who returns with nothing but horror stories about how rude and ignorant the men are, is a matter of cultural sensitivity.

It is easy to say, "I'm an evolved Westerner and I'll dress and behave any way I please," and most tourists do have exactly that attitude. But be aware of the consequences. People around the world are judged by how they dress and behave, as they are in the West. In many places, a woman who dresses too casually, and that can mean just wearing jeans and a t-shirt, is "available" and "easy." This is about as correct and as reasonable as saying a woman wearing a hijab in France is a terrorist, but unless you are ready to fight the cultural battles and deal with all the accompanying tension those entail, consider carefully how you may appear to the locals.

While in culturally conservative regions of the world, like the Middle East and South Asia, look at what the local women are wearing and adopt their custom. Some critics may say this is selling out to oppression or losing your "identity." However, in most cases the mode of dress is a cultural thing—conservative or otherwise—and observing local customs may very well ensure a more rewarding traveling experience.

The type of dress that is appropriate for women changes from country to country, but usually means covering the arms, wearing a shirt that covers the waist down to the thighs (with pants on), and sometimes covering the hair.

Women who choose to travel alone should also be aware that they are taking more chances than men who travel alone and thus need to be more careful. A seemingly innocent invitation for dinner to someone's home can end up a disaster. Women need to be very aware of vibes and trust their instincts when alone. Trust your instincts: If there is any feeling of a threat to your well-being, leave the scene immediately. It is better to be safe than sorry.

Relationships

Relationships between people vary in the way they manifest and are expressed in different parts of the world. The relationships between family members, different socio-economic and religious classes (or castes), and interpersonal relations differ more significantly than they do in most countries of the West.

An entire book could be written on this topic alone, but the best advice in learning this complex issue is simply to be observant. Watch, listen, and when in doubt, ask.

If you are on the road for any length of time, there is a good chance that you will meet someone in a host country and form a relationship with him/ her. This can be a very rewarding experience and an opportunity to gain valuable insights into the culture that would otherwise be inaccessible, but it also can create problems and challenges.

In many countries, especially in the poorer parts of the world, many of the people are looking for an opportunity for a ticket out. This doesn't mean that the person who falls in love with you is only putting on a show for an exit visa and an allowance. If expectations can form under false pretenses, the results may cause severe heart-break for both of you.

You will find that just being exotically different will make you an attractive target for many locals, especially in those parts of the world where such relationships are more relaxed. If you fall into this category, don't let all the attention go to your head. It is all right to appreciate it but be aware of what is going on. What may seem to you as a casual encounter could mean the world to the person you are with. As a sensitive traveler, you won't want to leave too many broken hearts in your wake. Bill Wilson, co-founder of Alcoholics Anonymous, once summed it up succinctly when he said, "to the world you may be one person but to one person you may be the world."

Always keep in mind the unique values and social climate of the culture you're immersing yourself in and think about how your behavior might be perceived by those around you.

While relationships between men and women are kept to a seemingly cool indifference in public in some parts of the world, relationships between men in those places are much closer. It is not uncommon to see Arab men holding hands in the Middle East. This does not mean they are gay—they would probably be very insulted if you voiced that assumption. As a Westerner staying with friends in the Middle East, it could take time to get used to this cultural trait. But if you are a man and are walking down the street with a male friend you recently met, don't be shocked if he reaches out to hold your hand. He is probably not making a pass. If that is his intention, he will probably stretch out his index finger while holding your hand and lightly scratch your palm. Men and women, on the other hand, never walk hand in hand in public. If you meet someone of the opposite sex and have a relationship in that part of the world, keep it discreet and in private.

In short, do your homework

When you're visiting a different country for the first time, there's always a risk of offending the locals by failing to observe customs that are normal for them or by not being aware of some of the aspects of your own culture that might be considered rude or out of place (for example, kissing your partner on the street in San Francisco compared to kissing her or him on the street in Cairo). Always keep in mind the unique values and social climate of the culture you're immersing yourself in and think about how your behavior might be perceived by those around you.

Given the complexity and sensitivity involved with cultural considerations around the world, again, it is essential to do some rigorous research before you head out. There are numerous sources online as well as good old-fashioned guidebooks that typically have a thoughtful section or two about local culture, taboos, and things to watch out for. You may also want to read through some travel blogs written by other visitors from around the world to get their take on a particular place and its culture.

Never forget that one region of a country might be tolerant or even permissive while another is less so (between big cities and rural areas, for example). The cultural reality in a resort where you can dress and behave casually, will obviously be much different from outside the resort, where very different standards apply.

Some cultural norms are interesting and relatively benign if you violate them. In the Middle East, you may notice that women never put their purse on the floor as this is considered to be bad luck. If you drop your purse on the floor, don't be surprised if someone comes over and picks it up for you.

To avoid the more serious forms of cultural faux pas, it is very important to do some research beforehand whether it's online, in books, or by talking to people from the country. Then, when in the country, try to be as sensitive and aware of details as possible. If you are walking down the street in shorts and notice that none of the locals are wearing shorts and are looking at you as an outsider, then perhaps you might want to consider changing. While I can highlight a few of the obvious examples in this book, your research might turn up all kinds of specific issues depending on the country. Perhaps taking photos of locals is considered offensive or the country has rigid blasphemy laws against certain types of speech. Knowing these ahead of time will help you avoid getting into uncomfortable or even illegal situations that could ruin your day, your trip, or perhaps even your life.

5:

Experiencing Nature

"Nature is man's teacher. She unfolds her treasures to his search, unseals his eye, illumes his mind, and purifies his heart; an influence breathes from all the sights and sounds of her existence."

— *Alfred Billings Street*

"Every land has its own special rhythm, and unless the traveler takes the time to learn the rhythm, he or she will remain an outsider there always."

— *Juliette de Baircli-Levi*

Eco-travel is becoming increasingly popular as the world undergoes a dramatic shift in consciousness regarding the environment .

Philipe Cirilo, a guide at Ariau Towers (a boutique hotel northwest of Manaus, Brazil, on the Rio Negro), guides a group of travelers through the dense tropical overgrowth of the Amazon rainforest while a cacophony of crickets, birds, and assorted creatures of the night fills the air with the primordial sounds of unadulterated nature. Overhead, an impressive stellar expanse blankets the firmament with an infinitude of stars and planets. An airborne fish suddenly lands in the boat but is carefully retrieved and thrown back in the water.

Suddenly, Cirilo jumps overboard yelling "I see one!" Silence. The sounds of the jungle resonate across the disturbingly still water. He suddenly surfaces with a small alligator in hold, tossing it carefully into the boat without losing a grip on its long intimidating jaws.

In the boat are three Americans, three Italians, and two Japanese, all on what is popularly known as an eco-tour. The midnight outing, referred to as an "alligator spotting" was but a small part of an experience that allowed the group to gain comfortably close access to raw nature.

After an introduction to the alligator, it was returned to the water, where it vanished without hesitation into the darkness.

—

When you quiet your mind to a point where thoughts subside into stillness and listen to the nature around you, you may find that every ecosystem and each natural place carries its own personality, its own vibration. Close your eyes and you may find that each place "feels" different. Take a long walk alone on a quiet beach, letting the sound of the waves wash over your consciousness. If you are able, hike up that trail to a mountain peak with a spectacular view on the valley below. Lay under a giant tree and watch the clouds move across the blue sky through the branches overhead. Then slowly sit up and hug that tree. Yes, hug that tree, and don't worry if someone might see you. This is what I call the third dimension of Intrepid Travel: Connecting with nature and the eco-systems of the countries you visit. You will undoubtedly discover that when you tune into nature, each ecosystem around the world resonates differently. Take the time to tune in; you won't regret it.

As previously mentioned in the chapter on Soulful Travel, it may be of no coincidence that the founders of the great religions, before reaching out to others and sharing their insights, spent a significant amount of time listening to nature. In the sixth century BC, Siddhartha Gautama, having slipped out of the confines of his father's palace in Lumbini, sat under a tree in the forest for seven days without moving before reaching the point he later called Nirvana. Six centuries later, Jesus of Nazareth walked into the desert for forty days, and six centuries after that the prophet Mohammed found himself a nice, quiet cave in which to sit and ponder the meaning of life.

Eco-traveling

Eco-travel is becoming increasingly popular as the world undergoes a dramatic shift in consciousness regarding the environment. Travelers are a socially conscious people with a concern for life, and it is natural for many of them to be aware of how their behavior affects not only their hosts, but their host country as well.

Ecological concerns are noticeably absent in many developing countries. There are places where environmentalism is not even part of the vocabulary. You'll be surprised at how impeccably clean some families in some places keep their homes, but only a few feet from their front step is a pile of decaying garbage over which hums a cloud of flies. This, however, is slowly changing, and since the early 1990s environmentalism has taken root in communities throughout the world.

There are two ways travelers can be ecologically minded and involved when on the road. The first is by exhibiting a concern for the environment, and the second is by joining an organized eco-tour. By publicly exhibiting a concern for the environment, the traveler sows seeds of awareness. He or she might even get a few of the locals to start thinking about how their behavior is affecting the planet. Take an exception to the "when in Rome" philosophy and carry your plastic bag to a garbage can or recycling bin (assuming there is one).

Eco-traveling as a way of life

Set a good example for other travelers and tourists. If you see someone throw an empty can on the ground, politely ask him to be more respectful.

Don't encourage poaching by buying parts of animals that should be left on the animals. Ivory is the most common, but you will be surprised at what unscrupulous salesmen will attempt to sell you in some parts of the world. Elephant feet, mountain gorilla hands, and the skins of zebras are but a few examples.

By enjoying the natural beauty this planet has to offer and doing it in a way that does not pollute the environment or exploit local communities, you are engaged in a form of independent eco-traveling. Trek through the Himalayas, kayak down the Baja peninsula, or bicycle around Europe. All these activities have minimal environmental impact. When you "take only pictures and leave only footprints," you are eco-traveling.

By enjoying the natural beauty this planet has to offer you are engaged in a form of independent eco-traveling.

On your own

Just about anywhere in the world there are opportunities to get out and experience nature. The opportunities range from rugged hikes to relaxing safaris. Nepal is one of the more popular trekking destinations. You don't even need to bring any gear; you can rent it all in Kathmandu or Pokhara. Once you have your gear, you get a permit to hike the trail of your choice. Along most of the routes there are villages about six or eight hours apart, each with a range of accommodation options.

In the European Alps, you can trek through some of the most magnificent and natural scenery this planet has to offer, staying in huts, cabins, village hotels or camping in designated areas along the way. As this book goes to press, I am in the middle of a 250 kilometer hike from Chamonix, in France, to Zermatt, in Switzerland. It is taking longer than anticipated because I am spending time in each village to talk with local French and Swiss villagers.

Any visit to East Africa would not be complete without a hike up Kilimanjaro. You can rent all your gear in Arusha, Moshi, or at the base of the mountain. There are no villages along the trail, so you should pack enough food for three or more days, a tent, stove, and a sleeping bag. There are camps along the main trail, but if you want to avoid the crowds, I would recommend a variation of the standard route.

The hike up Kilimanjaro begins in the jungle with monkeys swinging from the trees high above your head. You then slowly climb upwards through several different vegetation belts, until you reach the glaciers at over 20,000 feet (5,895 meters).

On the last day of the ascent, you leave base camp at midnight and reach the summit at dawn where you can watch the sun rise over the Indian Ocean, nearly four miles below you, while the ancient ice crunches underfoot.

If you plan to climb Kili, I would suggest going with the Kilimanjaro Initiative (KI), which organizes annual ascents to the summit while supporting and working with local communities. KI was founded as a nongovernmental organization (NGO) in Kenya in 2006 to encourage young women and men to have self-confidence and to assist in providing opportunities that will enable them to take on constructive roles in their communities. The climb helps raise awareness of social issues youth face in their communities and exemplifies how sport is used as a tool toward the development of a community. Visit the Kilimanjaro Initiative website for further information (kiworld.org/).

Also in East Africa, Mount Kenya offers a good challenge for the hardy hiker. Despite its location directly on the equator, the higher elevations are like the Swiss Alps. I once got lost in a snow storm there at 18,000 feet (5,500 meters) and had to bivouac on a scree slope of gravel until the sun came back up the next day.

Another good opportunity for trekking is in Peru. There, you can rent your equipment in Cusco if you don't have your own, and hike up the forty-five kilometer Inca trail to Machu Picchu, a journey that usually takes three days. All along the way there are ancient Inca ruins and villages of the descendants of the people who built them. The Inca Trail is one of the few places in the world where you can have the three-dimensional travel experience all at once. I hiked it alone under the light of a full moon, camping out within the walls of ancient Incan homes and religious temples.

For the adventurous, there is plenty of raw nature everywhere on earth to experience and appreciate, from the rainforests of the Amazon and the mountains of Nepal to the ice fields of Antarctica and the grasslands of Siberia. But hurry, Brazil is burning a football field of rainforest every second and ultraviolet rays are shining through the hole in the ozone layer and killing life at the southern pole.

Toxic waste is flowing into the oceans and acid rain is poisoning the lakes. Global temperatures are slowly rising, leading to rising sea levels and the disappearance of coastal landscapes.

If something is not done soon to halt the destruction our industrialized lifestyles are having on the environment, ours may truly be one of the last generations to explore and experience nature as we know it. What is needed is more people connecting with nature and then introducing that connection to others. We conserve only what we love, we love only what we understand, and we understand only what we experience. Through responsible travel we experience people, nature, and ourselves and we are more likely to do the right thing when it comes to our relationship with Mother Earth.

Joining an organized volunteer effort

Many travelers these days are looking for ways to combine the travel experience with a worthwhile project. A good way to get involved and make a difference is to join an organized volunteer effort with any of several organizations and companies around the world.

These eco-vacations are becoming increasingly popular. They offer an opportunity to travel, experience cultures, see beautiful scenery, and meet people. They also offer opportunities to contribute in some way towards the improvement of the environmental condition of our planet.

Organized eco-travel can take you to many of the same destinations as organized nature and adventure travel, with the bonus of directly benefiting conservation and the development of local economies. Through eco-travel, the traveler can visit some of the most spectacular scenery this planet has to offer, see rare and endangered species of wildlife, help them survive, and experience wonderful and exotic cultures.

An organized eco-vacation can be as rugged or relaxed as suits your personality. You can pitch in on an archeological dig in Israel, live with a family in India helping organize community action projects, or explore the natural beauty of the Galapagos Islands.

You can take a moonlit walk along Caribbean and South Pacific beaches to save the eggs of nesting turtles, observe caribou migrations in the outback of Alaska, assist on a scientific expedition to the North Pole, or accompany research projects to record the melodic communications of humpback whales. The possibilities are endless.

Carefully planned and organized tours that are ecologically correct are a great way to contribute toward the preservation of the planet's most beautiful areas. Conservation International, a nonprofit environmental organization headquartered in the U.S., says eco-tourism combines the pleasures of discovering spectacular flora and fauna with an opportunity to contribute directly to their

Carefully planned and organized tours are a great way to contribute toward the preservation of the planet's most beautiful areas.

protection. The organization considers eco-tourism to be one of the best ways of demonstrating quickly to developing countries that good conservation is also good business.

According to the World Tourism Organization, a branch of the United Nations headquartered in Madrid, eco-tourism refers to forms of tourism which have the following characteristics:

1. All nature-based forms of tourism in which the main motivation of the tourists is the observation and appreciation of nature as well as the traditional cultures prevailing in natural areas.
2. It contains educational and interpretation features.
3. It is generally, but not exclusively, organized by specialized tour operators for small groups. Service provider partners at the destinations tend to be small, locally-owned businesses.
4. It minimizes negative impacts upon the natural and socio-cultural environment.
5. It supports the maintenance of natural areas which are used as eco-tourism attractions by:
   » Generating economic benefits for host communities, organizations, and authorities managing natural areas with conservation purposes;
   » Providing alternative employment and income opportunities for local communities; *and*
   » Increasing awareness towards the conservation of natural and cultural assets, both among locals and tourists.

According to the latest figures from the UNWTO, tourism expanded and diversified over the past sixty years to become one of the largest and fastest-growing economic sectors in the world. Many new destinations have emerged in addition to the traditional favorites of Europe and North America. An ever-increasing number of destinations worldwide have opened up to and invested in tourism, turning it into a key driver of socioeconomic progress through the creation of jobs and enterprises, export revenues, and infrastructure development.

According to the World Travel and Tourism Council in its 2017 report on global economic impact of tourism, travel and tourism is a key sector for economic development and job creation throughout the world. In 2016, this sector directly generated US$2.3 trillion, creating 109 million jobs worldwide. Taking its wider indirect and induced impacts into account, the sector contributed US$7.6 trillion to the global economy and supported 292 million jobs in 2016. This was equal to 10.2 percent of the world's GDP, and approximately one in ten of all jobs.

And this growth is expected to continue: by 2027, the travel and tourism sector is expected to support more than 380 million jobs

Some institutions in Europe are working hard to preserve the planet's rich ecological heritage. Here, at Randers Rainforest in Denmark, Curator Ole Sommer Bach is trying to bring back pre-industrial flora and fauna to northern Europe.

globally, equating to one in nine of all jobs in the world. As a section of the global economic pie, the sector is expected to contribute around twenty-three percent of total global net job creation over the next decade.

These figures translate into tremendous financial incentive to cater to what those tourists would like to see and experience. Though eco-travel makes up only ten percent of all tourism, it is the fastest growing part of the tourism industry, expanding at more than thirty percent per year.

Many countries around the world are now taking heed of this advice and are profiting greatly from observing ecological concerns. Kenya and Costa Rica are two of the best examples. Kenya's numerous wildlife parks and preserves generated US$803 million in 2006, up from US$699 million the previous year.

For eco-tours to be successful, they need to be carefully managed. Mismanaged tours can be more destructive than they are helpful. When large numbers of visitors descend upon biologically and culturally sensitive areas, the effects can be devastating.

Many of the world's most beautiful areas have already been ruined by too many visitors, too little management, bad facilities, and improper disposal of waste. Some of this is done by tourists who consider themselves to be environmentalists. Dwight Holing, in the book, *Earth Trips*, calls this a case of "nature lovers loving nature to death."

In Nepal, Holing cites statistics of fifty thousand tourists trekking well-trodden routes to Mount Everest, leaving deforestation, litter, and soil erosion in their wake. The Inca Trail to Machu Picchu in Peru has seen the passing of modern-day Hansels and Gretels leaving trails of film containers and candy wrappers through the beautiful Andes Mountains. Even the fragile ecosystems of Antarctica have not escaped the harmful effects of uncontrolled tourism: Seven thousand people per year now visit the polar ice cap.

6:

Getting Your Gear in Order

"Someone said to Socrates that a
certain man had grown no better from
his travels. 'I should think not,' he replied.
'He took himself along with him.'"

— *Michel de Montaigne*

What you should bring will depend on your needs and your itinerary—where you plan to go and what you will do when you get there.

You've made the big decision. You want to travel, to explore the world, and experience what there is beyond the horizon—and beyond that horizon that is just beyond the horizon. All you must do now is prepare yourself for the journey.

Preparation for travel is of two varieties: mental and physical. The first involves gaining knowledge of the places you plan to visit and learning some of the language. Tangible preparation consists of compiling what you will bring with you and getting all the necessary documentation. Both are equally important. We covered mental preparation in the previous chapters; here we move on to the nitty gritty of what to bring.

Passports and visas

Your passport will be the first official documentation that you acquire for your travels. If you are applying for the first time, you need to go to a passport agency in person. If there is not one in your city, a federal or state court may serve the same purpose. In smaller towns, a post office may accept applications.

When you receive your passport, memorize the number as well as the place and date of issue. Make two photocopies; leave one

at home and hide the other somewhere in your pack. Also, prepare copies of all your most important documents, including your
passport and health insurance, and digitally upload them to an
online safe storage site. I personally prefer the Swiss-based Secure-
Safe (www.securesafe.com), which is a "cloud vault" that protects
documents and passwords, offering a level of security comparable
to a Swiss bank. SecureSafe is a unique solution with a high level
of privacy protection. I believe their servers are even buried deep
within the Swiss Alps.

These simple precautions will save you a lot of time and trouble
if you need to have the passport replaced. If you lose your passport,
vaccination certificate, or need a copy of your birth certificate you
can go to an internet cafe, log in to SecureSafe, and print out them
out. Of course, with a passport you will need to take the copy to
your embassy to have it replaced, but it will be much easier if you
have a copy, rather than if you show up with just a story and a tear.

If your government allows for passports with extra pages, the general rule is this: It is better to have and not need, than to need and
not have. American passports used to have the advantage of getting
accordion page inserts, which were long folded strips of paper that
add new pages. After a few years, I had four or five of these accordion pages connected end to end that would stretch halfway across a
room when unfolded. It was indeed a novelty, but had its perils when
border guards and immigration officials wanted to carefully inspect
each visa stamp to determine how well it compared to their own, or
if they needed to ensure that I did not visit a country that was on
their list of enemies (for example, an entry stamp or visa from Israel
would disqualify you from visiting most Arab countries). The United
States then started to seal in extra pages that turned like a book. This
practice, however, was also discontinued in 2017. I was told at the
embassy in Zurich that I received one of the last exceptions.

If you are traveling to a country that requires a visa, you will need to apply for a visa at the consulate or embassy of the country you plan to visit (or High Commission if the country is a member of the British Commonwealth). Be sure to have a half-dozen pictures of yourself ready (they will probably only ask for two or three, but I have been asked for more). If you plan to travel for an extended period, you may want to consider bringing a few dozen photos of yourself. More about this process is discussed in the chapter on red tape and documentation.

What to bring

After getting all your documentation, passports, visas, etc., the next thing you will want to know is what to bring with you. The answer is, quite simply, as little as possible. Not only does carrying a heavy load become overwhelmingly burdensome, it makes it very difficult to maneuver in crowds and use public transportation in cities. Airlines are increasingly charging for checked baggage, so if you can fit everything into a carry-on, you can save money. If you plan to hitch rides as your means of transport, big loads make it difficult, especially in Europe where the cars are much smaller than in North America. Carrying large packs full of possessions also makes you a more likely target for thieves. What you don't have, you can't lose.

What you will decide to bring will depend on your needs and your itinerary—where you plan to go and what you will do when you get there. Most people usually start off with much more than they need and then discard things along the way; others start off with nearly nothing and then acquire a museum on their journey.

When I set off on my first around-the-world adventure, my pack was the largest on the shelf and I had it packed so full it was nearly bursting at the seams. I quickly learned I didn't need half of what I had brought and gradually reduced my load to the bare minimum while traveling through West Africa and across the Sahara.

A person I traveled with for a while in Africa claimed to have the minimum-load philosophy down to a science. He had only three socks and every time he took a shower, he would wash one and hang it up to dry. This way he kept them rotating around and every day (provided he showered), he had a clean sock.

Duffel bag, pack, or suitcase?

When choosing what to pack your possessions in, you need to consider versatility and convenience. A backpack is the luggage of choice for most travelers for the obvious ease of being able to throw your load upon your back and pack it around. This is especially useful if you do any hiking during your travels. A backpack, however, causes problems when you are trying to get on a bus, or move through a crowd and it keeps knocking people over. Additionally, when you are carrying a backpack, it is easier for a thief to sneak up behind you and start unloading your gear as you walk merrily along your way.

I now prefer a small duffel bag because I can easily sling it over my shoulder, and keep it close to my chest when moving through crowds (to avoid prying fingers). However, you can't climb Kilimanjaro carrying a duffel bag, or do a month's trekking in the Himalayas. If you go for the pack, hip straps are important. They keep the weight off your shoulders and distribute the weight more efficiently. Reflect upon your options and choose the gear that will best serve your purposes. Also, you can always trade out your gear while traveling and shift from pack to duffel bag to suitcase with wheels.

A recent development on the luggage scene is a backpack that converts to a duffel bag – I find these to be a great option although the back support is not as sturdy as it is with solid backpacks. These convertibles are great for airline travel and border crossings. Backpacks sometimes label the owner as a hippie or possibly a drug-user, and the inner frame convertible pack is a good way to get around this stereotype.

Another advantage with a duffel bag and the type of pack that converts into one is that they have zippers you can put a lock on. They may not stop a thief, but it will slow him down, which is usually enough to discourage him. The zipper should, however, be a sturdy one. Any zipper will break if too much pressure is put on it, so be sure not to pack in too much.

Pick a size sufficient for gear you plan to bring. If you go for the larger pack, be assured that you will try and fill it and soon will be overweighed with a lot of unnecessary possessions. If you choose to carry a suitcase, use one with wheels and be prepared for sore arms and a tired back when you do have to carry them up and down stairs. Their main advantage is that the hard-cased ones are difficult to break into.

Show me the money

Yes, you are going to need money. The amount you will need will depend for the most part on what countries you are in, your living requirements, and how long you plan to travel.

I find it is a good idea to keep an emergency stash somewhere back home with mom or a trusted friend that you can call upon if needed. This cash cache will help if you find yourself in a bind somewhere and need money to tide you over until you find work or it can buy you a plane ticket if you need to fly home right away. In the original edition of this book I suggested keeping $1,000 in reserve. These days it might be useful to have at least $3,000 or at least a spare credit card with that much as the limit.

If you are going to be traveling for extended periods of time, and exposing your gear to crowds, wear a money belt—the kind that fits inside your belt and up next to your skin. Everything you have of high value should be next to your skin always. Start wearing it a few days before you leave and get used to it being there. Besides carrying your money, your money belt will be used to stash your immunization certificate, credit cards, and any other important documentation that you can't afford to lose. While on the road, your money belt will be your lifeline. Place your traveler's checks, cash, credit cards,

Check ahead to see if you will need a power plug adapter or voltage converter for the power sockets (outlets) used at your destination.

etc. inside a zip-lock bag or something similar to prevent them from getting wet from your sweat while inside your money belt.

Credit cards are good security in case all goes wrong. Some cards offer good travel benefits. They can also be a good way to pay for the major expenses if you don't plan to be gone for long. If you plan to travel for a long time and will be using a credit card, you can set up an automatic monthly payment program at your bank.

The list

The following list is just meant to offer some ideas as a rough guideline that you will need to adapt to your own requirements. What you will need to bring will depend on where you are going and your personal needs.

Address book of family and friends: Make a copy of your address book to bring along with you. Do not bring the original in case something happens and you lose it. You can also use online address books, such as Google.

Business cards: Jim Rogers is an American businessman, investor, traveler, financial commentator, and author based in Singapore. In the early 1990s he traveled across Eurasia from London to Japan on a motorcycle looking for adventure and investment opportunities. He chronicled all this in the book *Investment Biker: Around the World with Jim Rogers*.

Even if you are not Jim Rogers and don't plan on seeking out investments or other business opportunities on your travels, it's still a good idea to bring along some business cards. If you do not have any, get some printed up. Not only are they good when applying for visas, they provide a convenient way to exchange addresses with people on the road. If you plan to do any travel writing on the road, cards can be useful. If you do not have a title, be creative. Freelance travel journalist is usually good, unless you are traveling in an area that does not welcome reporters. Being a travel writer can also get you better service at restaurants and room upgrades at hotels. Start a travel blog and Twitter feed and put that on your travel business card.

Camera: I recommend a small waterproof digital camera such as the COOLPIX W100 or Canon PowerShot D30. There will be more on photography in the next chapter.

Clothes: The clothes you choose to bring will depend for the most part on where you will be traveling and what you plan to do when you are there. If you are going to Europe and plan a lot of formal outings, you may need to bring formal or semi-formal slacks, shirts, and a jacket. For women you may want to consider, in addition, dresses and blouses. For backpackers I recommend two pairs of light cotton pants, a pair of dress pants, two T-shirts, two collar shirts, three or four pairs of underwear, three pairs of socks, a belt, swimsuit, and shorts. For the sake of comfort, all clothes should be pure cotton or wool for cooler climates. One set of good clothes is essential for border crossings.

Condoms: These may be difficult to find in some places, and those that are available may not be as safe or as satisfying as the ones you can find elsewhere. So, if you have a favorite brand, bring them in case of emergency. Again, the motto here is "Better to have and not need, than to need and not have."

Credit or debit cards: I never had credit cards during my early days of exploring, but now I wouldn't leave home without them. ATMs did not exist when I first started traveling, but now you can find them almost anywhere. The cards do have their advantages, with the main one being assurance that you won't run out of money. An American Express card entitles you to very convenient overseas services such as mail (which, of course, is less useful in the digital age). A pre-loaded debit card can be a good way to store money—and have someone deposit cash into an account back home in case you need quick access to it.

Daypack/rucksack: These are handy for daily outings or for short excursions from a base city. When flying, it is a good idea to carry your important valuables like camera equipment and film with you in a small rucksack instead of leaving them in your luggage.

First-aid kit: A first aid kit is an essential piece of equipment on any travel or backpacking adventure, but most travelers aren't sure exactly what they need to take with them. For this item, please see Chapter 10, Staying Healthy.

Flashlight and batteries: These are absolute essentials that you won't realize you'll need until you are stumbling through the dark. Flashlights are great for finding your way to the bathroom in the middle of the night.

Flip-flops (thongs): These are a must for most showers and for walks on the beach.

Glasses and contact lenses: Contacts are not a good idea when traveling as dust may cause them to irritate your eyes. Bring an extra pair of glasses and a copy of your prescription in case you lose or break them. For good measure put a copy of your prescription online at SecureSafe or another online digital repository. Some people leave a pair of glasses at home, ready to be sent out to them in the event of loss or breakage.

Guidebooks and phrasebooks: You'll be glad you brought these, but don't go overboard. Each book means more weight. You won't initially need to buy one for every country you plan to visit along your route. Travelers you meet along the way will trade you theirs of places they've been. And, of course, you can carry several of them on your tablet.

Handkerchiefs: Even if you have never carried one of these, you will find a lot of uses for one while on the road. Some examples: You can use one to blow your nose, for first-aid purposes, or to use as a sweatband.

Hat: Especially in tropical countries, the sun will take its toll on your head without a hat. A small cap usually works best and is the easiest to carry with you. If you don't have a hat, a handkerchief works well. If you are traveling in cold areas, remember that most of the body's warmth is lost through the top of the head.

Insect repellent: This is especially important for regions where malaria is prevalent. If you are traveling in an area with malaria and other insect-borne diseases, bring a few ounces of the best you can get your hands on. Look for something with a high DEET content, preferably around ninety percent. This is the chemical that repels mosquitoes.

Insurance: Types of insurance you will want to consider include trip cancellation insurance if you have a lot of money invested in a trip, travel and medical insurance, baggage loss insurance, and legal assistance insurance. Most are included in comprehensive insurance packages. Carefully consider what you do and do not need, and check any existing insurance coverage to determine if you are already covered. My father was recently on a round-the-world cruise when he had a heart attack in Barcelona. If he and my step-mother had not purchased the extra insurance the cruise line offered, the medical and evacuation costs would have run into the tens of thousands of dollars. After three weeks in the hospital (the cruise had to leave them in Spain), the insurance company sent out a private jet to pick them up and fly them back to the United States, where their normal health insurance took over.

International certificate of vaccination: Check with your family doctor to see what, if any, inoculations are required where you are going. Your doctor should be able to get the official certificate that records when and where you received your shots. The international certificate is designed to reduce the spread of illness around the world by unvaccinated travelers. At many border crossings, you will be asked for one. If you don't have one, they may require that you get your shots at the border before being allowed into the country, which may expose you to risk of contamination if the needles are not clean.

International driver's license: If you plan to do any driving while overseas, get one of these. They are available from your local Automobile Association and are good for one year.

International student identity card: If you qualify, get one before you go. It will save you money on everything from museums to airplane tickets. Officially you must be a full-time student to get one, but in some places, like Greece and Hong Kong, you can buy one with very little proof. The card is a creation of the International Student Travel Confederation (ISCTC), which has members in seventy-four countries. The ISTC was established in 1949 by university student unions to make travel affordable for students. Today more than seventy specialist student travel companies work through the not-for-profit member associations of the ISTC to further this goal. They specialize in securing student benefits in the areas of flights, insurance, ground transport, work exchange programs, and international identity cards. The ISTC network includes more than 5,000 offices in over 200 countries. Members collectively serve ten million students each year. To obtain an International Student Identity Card, apply at your local school or university with proof of enrollment or contact them online at www.aboutistc.org.

Knife: Yes, MacGyver was right—never leave home without your trusted Swiss Army knife. It will prove to be your best friend no matter where you're going. With a Swiss Army knife you can open a can, slice bread, cut cheese, punch a hole in your belt if you've lost weight from your travels, mend your shoes, remove a sliver from your finger, pick spinach from your teeth, open a bottle of wine, and cut paper. Just remember that you can no longer carry a pocket knife onto an airplane, so if you have one you will need to check in your luggage. I learned this one the hard way, sacrificing many good Swiss Army knives at airport security.

Laundry soap: Depending on where you are traveling, it can be useful to have a bit of laundry detergent to wash laundry in the bathtub, especially when you want clean socks and underwear.

Luggage tags: Get something sturdy that cannot be easily torn off. I like the leather ones you can slip your business card in.

Maps: It is always helpful to know where you are in relation to other places around you. I prefer hard copy and often carry a map of the world, one of the region, and a map of the country. Since maps are sometimes difficult to find on the road, bring them with you from home. Nowadays you can download maps from Google on your smartphone. If you prefer this option, be sure to download the maps while connected to a Wi-Fi, so you can access them later.

Mosquito net: This is essential if you're traveling to the tropics. One of these can make the difference between a good night's sleep and a restless one. They are also essential in avoiding malaria. Many hotels in the tropics do have them, but it can be a good idea to bring your own just in case. There are some lightweight ones on the market today that do not take up much room in your pack. Look for them at your local outdoors or army surplus store.

Notebooks and pens: I keep three notebooks—one for addresses of people I meet on the road, another for information gleaned from fellow travelers, and a third for my own personal journal. Be sure to keep an accurate diary of your experiences; it makes for excellent reading on those long bus trips and the details can be transferred into an online blog or journal. These days some people prefer a tablet. If you choose this option be sure to send backups of your notes to an email server in case you lose it.

Passport: You can't leave home without one.

Passport photos: It's good to stock up on these because you will need them when applying for visas on the road. I replenish my supply every chance I can and try to keep about a dozen with me always.

Power adaptors and transformers: Check ahead to see if you will need a power plug adapter or voltage converter for the power sockets (outlets) used at your destination. The EU now has more or less all conformed to the same standard, except for Switzerland and Britain. When traveling around the world, you can either get adaptors for each country, or opt for the all-in-one, which looks like a small round cannister. Some of the better ones even come with USB ports.

Important: be careful about plugging in your devices without checking on the voltage. The adaptor only changes the shape of the plug itself – if you plug in a device meant for 120 volts in the US into a European socket with 230 volts, it will mostly likely fry. Most phones, laptops, and cameras now run on either 120 or 230. Check the small print on the back of the device before attempting to plug it in. If you absolutely need that electronic device that runs on 120 volts, you will need to get a step-down travel transformer to convert the electricity.

The only true universal power source is the lighter socket in the car. Very few people use them to light their cigarettes, but they do make a very useful power source. I have used them to charge my video camera batteries while shooting a documentary in Mozambique, and then for boiling a cup of water for tea. They are also indispensable for keeping your smart phone charged while on the road. I find the best device for charging USB devices to be the RAVPower RP-VC006 because it has the right balance of all the important features at a good price (around $10). It can simultaneously charge two smartphones at 2.4 amps each (more than twice the speed of the built-in USB ports found in most cars).

Radio: If you are the kind of person who wants to stay in touch with the world, there are some remarkably small shortwave radios on the market today. Also, if you can get Wi-Fi, there are some great news and music apps available for download. Wherever I am in the world, I start the day with a stream of news from the BBC, NPR, CBC, and Euronews. The world has changed so much since the first edition of this book was published in 1992 when getting world news while traveling was much more difficult (although that may have been a good thing).

Sewing kit: Include safety pins, half a dozen needles, spare buttons, and about four small spools of different colored thread to match the color of your clothing.

Sleeping bag: Whether to carry a sleeping bag depends for the most part on where you are going. Obviously, if you are going to hike through the Andes, it would be a good idea to have one. But if you plan on boating down the Amazon, all you'll need is a sheet and a hammock. If you need a sleeping bag, try to avoid getting one filled with down. Down sleeping bags are useless when they get wet. A better option is a polyester fiber-fill such as Hollofil or Qualofil, which will keep its heat even if it gets wet. If you are not going to be traveling in cold areas, you may find it useful to make yourself a sleepsack. Take a simple twin size sheet, and fold it over. Sew the bottom together and around three-quarters up the side, and voila! instant sleepsack. Always carry one of these when staying in budget hotels in Developing countries. Sheets are rarely provided and even when they are, you will probably not want to use them.

Small lock with two keys: Some of the more budget-oriented hotels may not have a lock on the door, but a latch, into which you can put your own padlock. This is a lot better than a door lock where you cannot be sure who will come in while you are out. Have the extra key in case you team up with another traveler and share a room. You should also have one to lock the zippers on your pack shut.

Smartphone: The smartphone may very well be your most vital travel tool: You can rely on it for navigating unfamiliar places, finding places to eat and things to do, and taking photos. If you bring one, don't forget to bring a small, lightweight external battery pack. My battery pack of choice is the Anker PowerCore Slim – it is small and capable of charging a smartphone two times.

I sometimes carry two phones – one with an international roaming plan from my home country, and another into which I can insert a local sim card (which gives me a local number, but also much lower data fees). The second phone of course needs to be unblocked.

Stuffsacks: Great for the first-aid kit, toiletries, sewing kit, peanuts, anything!

Sunscreen: Bring both the kind for tanning and some sunblock for your face. When you spend a day at the ruins or even walking along the beach, you could end up with a serious sunburn if you do not have sunscreen.

Tablet (iPad or otherwise): Can be useful for taking notes (see above), for doing research, storing books, video chats, etc. If you bring a smartphone, you may not also need a tablet – but it is worth considering as the screen is much larger.

Tent: Very useful if you plan on doing extensive backcountry hiking.

Tiger balm: This lifesaver is listed in the first-aid section, but deserves a mention of its own because of its importance. Tiger balm is effective for headaches, sore muscles, and to soothe itchiness from mosquito bites.

Toiletries: Bring a toothbrush, toothpaste, comb, small shampoo bottle (buy a couple of these to be reused), deodorant, razor (if you want to shave), soap, and a small towel. Bring toilet paper if you are traveling to Africa, The Middle East, or India, and you think you absolutely cannot adapt to local custom (water).

Valuables pouch and a money belt: These are essential if you want to hang on to your money and important documents.

Water bottle: More than 100 million plastic bottles are used worldwide every day and can take more than 400 years to degrade. Be sure to have a reusable water bottle, especially if you're going to hot climates. In areas with unsafe water you will need a water bottle to mix your water with purification tablets. New to hit the market are water bottles that double as filtration—such as the Hydros coconut-based carbon filter, which is good for 150 uses, or the CamelBak's bottle, which claims a spill-proof design.

Watch/alarm: Alarm clocks are an absolute necessity for catching that early morning train or plane. Have a backup besides your phone just in case.

Ziploc bags: Keep a few of these handy; they're great for waterproofing things like your camera when traveling in wet areas and to keep your money and documents in while inside your money belt.

7:

Photography: Capturing a Thousand Words

"You don't take a photograph, you make it."
— *Ansel Adams (1902 – 1984)*

How you compose your photos will make all the difference between a snapshot and an image that will replace a thousand words.

Traveling offers innumerable opportunities to take pictures. While traveling, you will no doubt want to document your journey for posterity or simply to share with the folks back home. Some people collect souvenirs when they travel. My favorite souvenirs are those implied by the English meaning of that French word—memories. And nothing brings back a memory more than a good photograph.

Travel photography is like a time machine, freezing memories from a journey that you can look back on and enjoy for years. This chapter is meant to share some of my own insights into travel photography gained from my many years traveling with a camera, both as a traveler and as a photographer for the United Nations, where I visited at least fifty countries shooting still imagery and video documentaries.[5]

When traveling, always be sensitive to local beliefs about photography. If the locals believe that you will steal a part of their soul by taking their picture, do not take their picture. If they see you aiming at them through your lens, their belief will make it a reality for them. Once in the central African country of Burundi, while hiking through the hills from Tanzania, I stopped at a small hamlet to talk to a group of locals. One of them was working on a sewing machine

---

5   www.flickr.com/photos/adamrogersundp/

in the most austere surroundings. I thought to myself that would make a beautiful picture, but when I pulled my camera out, he started yelling "You want to steal me!"

How does one respond to that other than apologizing and putting the camera away?

Choosing a camera

Ansel Adams once said, "there's nothing worse than a sharp image of a fuzzy concept." What I think he meant was don't focus on the equipment so much that you forget about that which matters most: Always remember to put your vision and creativity first, and then let the tools follow.

That said, if you have nothing to shoot with, then all the vision and creativity in the world will come to naught. In the first two editions of this book, I recommended a 35mm SLR (Single Lens Reflex) for capturing images. The world has changed, and you no longer need to carry film and worry about it being spoiled by x-ray machines at the airport. I now recommend a small waterproof digital camera such as the COOLPIX W100 or Canon PowerShot D30. Another option that my fellow travel photographers are using is the micro four thirds camera. They are small, very lightweight, and have the ability to swap lenses. Both Panasonic and Olympus are making some great cameras and lenses with the traveler in mind.

As the skills of a photographer are much more important than the camera itself, a lot can be said for the images you can capture with a smartphone such as the Samsung Galaxy or the iPhone. The cameras on smartphones have come a long way since their humble beginnings and now can compete with sophisticated cameras when in the hands of a skilled photographer.

If you choose to shoot with your phone, and want to add even more capacity, you may want to consider a clip-on lens. Smartphone camera lenses can go beyond what you get with a traditional phone camera. For example, they offer telephoto and zoom, or capture wide-angle shots in fisheye, or hone in on the tiny details of a subject. Clip on lenses come in all shapes and sizes, and many companies manufacture them. For example, the Comsun 5-in-1 Universal Clip-on Cell Smartphone Camera Lens Kit retails for about ten dollars on Amazon and comes with a 235-degree Fisheye, a 0.4X Wide Angle, a 19X Macro, a 2X barlow, and even comes with a circular polarizing filter (CPL).

The downside to shooting with your phone is that most smartphones that shoot good images are expensive and taking them out to take pictures could expose you as a target for theft.

Subject, composition, and light

At its base, a camera is just a tool for capturing light. Much more important than the camera are the skills, insights, and sensibilities of the photographer. Even as the technology of photography is advancing so rapidly that you don't even have to focus anymore, the impact and quality of an image will always depend on three things: subject, composition, and light.

The subject

Photographing people in other countries can be a challenge for many photographers. One must communicate and consider whether or not they may get offended. It took me a couple years to get comfortable shooting portraits of people in other countries.

Remember it is the unique places, people, food, crafts, and customs that make our travel photos so captivating. A sunset with warm light is fine if you have a silhouette of something that is indicative of the place you are in. For example, an acacia tree silhouetted against the fiery ball of sun descending over the Serengeti. Nothing is more boring than looking at your fellow travelers' sunset photos when they return from a trip because they could have stayed home and shot the orange sunset and clouds.

In general, if you want to capture that magical moment with your camera, you will need to be as discrete as possible. If you are going to travel with more than a compact camera, carry your equipment in an inconspicuous camera bag that is easy to conceal. Some of the best ones are the Domke bags, invented by a professional newspaper photographer, Jim Domke. They offer the most versatility and durability for the traveler.

The reason for being discrete is twofold: Firstly, you do not want to attract the attention of a thief, and secondly, as a traveler, you are trying to blend in as much as possible. The idea is to cross the line between "us" and "them," and flaunting lots of camera equipment sometimes makes this difficult.

Having stated all that, the best shots are taken in natural settings, with the subject unaware that his or her picture is being taken. It is a tough call to make. If you are spotted and the subject starts to get upset, quietly put your camera away and try as best as possible to make friends. Explain that you only want your family back home to see the same beauty that you are there witnessing.

I usually avoid posed pictures because only those so trained act naturally in front of the lens. The rest of us stiffen up and get self-conscious when on center stage. If you are shooting posed subjects, talk to them and help them to relax and forget what you are doing. The best photographs are a result of a combination of equipment, film, lighting and the photographer.

The key is to talk to people first and to get them to be comfortable with you. Look them in the eye and smile from the heart. Say hello. Ask for directions. Buy a souvenir. Compliment them on something. Chat for a few minutes *before* asking for a photo. This approach will be far less invasive. If they say no—no means no. Put your camera away and say "Thank you. No problem."

The composition

How you compose your photos will make all the difference between a snapshot and an image that will replace a thousand words. It will also be the cornerstone in the development of your own voice in photography. I can offer a few hints and general principles here, but how you develop your style will depend on what you do with them.

Find that unique angle

Most photos are shot from chest height of a standing adult. This may be the most convenient way of taking a photo, but there are usually more creative options. One is to get down low and situate something interesting in the foreground, especially if you are using a wide-angle lens.

Especially when photographing children, you should always bring the camera down to their eye level or below. Looking down on kids from the perspective of an adult very rarely makes for good or interesting photos. Go down on your knees and connect with the children human to human. Get them to feel comfortable with you and play with them. Cross your eyes or pretend to fall.

You can compose your shot through the frame of an old window, through the leaves of a tree, with your feet framing the edges—the sky is the limit. The idea is to be creative and to offer a perspective that others seldom even consider.

Rule of thirds

The rule of thirds is perhaps the most basic and classic of all photography tips and one that will help you create more balanced compositions. Imagine breaking an image down into thirds horizontally and vertically, so it's split into different sections.

The goal is to place important parts of the photo into those sections and help frame the overall image in a way that's pleasing to the eye. The theory is that if you place points of interest in the intersections or along the lines, your photo will be more balanced and will enable a viewer of the image to interact with it more naturally. Apparently, studies have shown that people's eyes usually go to one of the intersection points most naturally rather than the center of the shot. Thus, although a technical rule based on empirical studies, using the rule of thirds promotes a natural way of viewing an image.

For example, place a person along the left grid line rather than directly in the center, or consider keeping your horizon on the bottom third, rather than splitting the image in half.

In the beginning, until you develop a habit, try turning on your camera's "grid" feature, which displays a rule of thirds grid directly on your LCD screen specifically for this purpose. If shooting a portrait, line up your subject's eyes on the top third horizontal line. In addition, keep the rule of thirds in mind as you edit your photos later on. Post-production editing software has good tools for cropping and re-framing images so that they fit within the rules.

Once you have gotten comfortable with this rule, find creative ways to break it. This may sound counterintuitive, but knowing the rules is important to being able to break them, resulting in dynamic, creative, and powerful photography.

The light

Light is probably the most important factor for great photography. You have the soft, warm morning light that creates amazing subtle images and the high-contrast mid-morning and late afternoon/evening light that brings out the best contrast and warmest color tones. The worst time of course is high noon, with the direct sun overhead that washes out all contrast. I have been in many situations around the world where I needed to photograph specific subjects, but I arrived at 11 a.m. and had to engage the people I wanted to photograph and keep them in conversation until the sun descended lower toward the horizon. This was usually better anyway, as after a few hours of discussion the subjects—often farmers planting rice or women marketeers selling vegetables—were comfortable with my presence.

High-quality video production tools are now extremely affordable and within reach to just about everyone.

With darker-skinned subjects, set your exposure accordingly. These are often the most difficult photographs to take, especially if the background is bright. An important caveat to remember is shoot one photo with what your meter says, then shoot a photo one aperture over and another with one aperture under. An aperture also is called an f-stop. Overexposing slightly (open the aperture up a f-stop to allow more light to strike the digital sensor—f-11 allows very little light, whereas f-2.8 allows a lot) will bring more detail into the darker areas of your photograph. Another trick is to move close to your subject and meter on his or her face and record the meter reading. Then move back to compose your photograph and shoot. You may also want to consider the exposure compensation dial if you are using an automatic mode. This is the feature on your camera with the +/- button. Once you press this button it will allow you to dial in the compensation that you need to lighten or darken your next shot.

Shooting video

More and more travelers are bringing small, compact video cameras with them when traveling or are filming with their smartphones. Unless you are working on a specific project to film a specific event, I would not recommend this. Video cameras make you very conspicuous and a target for theft. Plus, they often make people uncomfortable. With video, you cannot simply take a photograph and put your camera away but must keep your camera pointed at your subjects until your segment is complete.

That said, high-quality video production tools are now extremely affordable and within reach to just about everyone. I have seen some amazing travel documentaries produced with nothing more than an iPhone and iVideo.

8:

Transportation: Getting from A to B, Then All the Way to Z

"To travel hopefully is a better thing than to arrive. Enjoy your journey; don't rush it. Check out the side trips and smell the roses."

— *Robert Louis Stevenson*

Traveling by boat is one of the most enjoyable, therapeutic, and peaceful forms of transportation available.

Transportation

You've gathered your gear, prepared yourself mentally, and have obtained all the necessary documentation for your trip. The next step is to take the step. Most travelers in the United States and Canada begin their long-awaited journey with a trip to the airport and then venture off overland from wherever they land.

While traveling from A to B, try to experience C to Z. Try picking a destination on a map, and then look for the most difficult route (or most poetic) to get there. This method will always make the trip interesting. Then take a different route back to complete a loop, ensuring that all along the way you are en route and exploring.

When traveling, I find it useful to have a purpose, such as birdwatching, learning a local dialect, studying ancient ruins, etc. Do not just wander around aimlessly. Having a direction not only keeps your mind focused on an objective, but it goes over a lot better with the locals, and even more importantly, with the police. I have had some incredible experiences in very remote rural areas in countries as diverse as Bangladesh and Syria, but I always had a destination (usually an old ruin or a temple in the area). In the words of the Egyptian/Greek poet Constantine Peter Cavafy: As you set out for Ithaka; hope your road is a long one, full of adventure, full of discovery.

In other words, getting to places such as Ithaca can be as much or even more interesting than the destination itself. With map in hand, set out on local transport to some lost ruin or grotto—or even better, walk and ask people along the way. The locals will be proud to show them off to you and will probably take you into their homes afterwards.

Itineraries

It is a good idea to know where you are going but try not to have an itinerary that is too rigid. One of the great joys of traveling is not having to adhere to a fixed schedule. The tighter your time restriction, the less you will enjoy the journey. This is especially true in some countries in the tropics where time takes on an entirely new meaning. Relax, enjoy yourself, take your watch off (or better yet, leave it at home). Stay open to fluctuations in plans. New opportunities will constantly present themselves—new sites to visit, ruins to explore, and people to spend time with. If you are on a tight schedule (Paris today, Rome tomorrow), you will undoubtedly miss out on many golden opportunities.

Always try to plan your travel as a loop, not as a point A to point B and back to A again linear journey. That way, the journey will be as interesting as the destinations, and you will have more places to visit. For example, if in Paris, and traveling to Marseille, consider going to Lyon, then to Marseille, then back to Paris by way of Toulouse and Nantes.

If you are limited with your time, try not to see too much. It is better to experience what you have time to experience with depth rather than to gain superficial exposure in a whirlwind tour. If you are working and must beg and plead with your boss for that extra two weeks, do it. You won't regret it. If you are a student leaving for the summer, don't waste any time after finals. Be ready the day after and plan to get back just before the fall semester.

You will be able to figure out how you will get around when you get there. Experiment with a variety of modes of transport. Don't listen to the people who tell you that if you don't reserve your place on the tour coach before you leave home you'll miss out. Just ask around to find out how the locals get to where you want to go. They do it all the time!

Online travel services

One of the greatest benefits of the age of the internet is the ability to go online and compare prices, sign up for e-specials, and track your miles for free tickets. Each airline has a website and a smartphone app, often offering point bonuses for booking on your iPhone or Android device. At one time, travel agencies were the only way to plan your trip. Now, you can plan your trip online, compare prices, and book your travel plans.

The best online travel sites ensure you get the most for your money within your budget. They also help you make the most of every minute when you are on vacation. These sites make it easy to quickly organize every facet of your trip: flights, lodging, and any short trips in between. But beware—some dishonest companies create legitimate-looking websites with official-sounding names, and instead of doing what you pay them for, they take your money and disappear. Therefore, user reviews, especially those from TripAdvisor.com, are valuable because you see if other travelers have had a negative experience using a particular online travel site.

While in Rwanda on a work trip in January 2018 I wanted to book a trip to the Virunga National Park across the border in the Democratic Republic of the Congo. I read a traveler's report on a local website, called LivinginKigali.com, run by some local expats. The report drew my attention to the Netflix documentary called Virunga, which I promptly watched on my iPhone while eating a meal at a local restaurant on the border. It also pointed my attention to the park's website, VisitVirunga.org, endorsing its authenticity. On VisitVirunga.org I was able read more reviews and interact with staff and then book the park fees, transport from the border, and gear for the climb. With just a few clicks of the mouse I organized a memorable hike up Nyiragongo volcano to see the world's largest lake of boiling lava.

The plane truth about flying

In the age of the internet, and a plentitude of travel sites offering reduced-rate fares, it is getting cheaper and cheaper to fly. Always check different sites, from Travelocity to Expedia, as well as the websites of the different airlines. Keep in mind the frequent flier families, such as One World or Star Alliance as concentrating your miles can bring benefits later in the form of free tickets. This comes in handy at check-in counters, and in access to their lounges during international travel.

Even if you are unable to get a special bargain price, there are probably a half-dozen different fares, ranging from economy to first class. Excursion fares are usually offered on long flights with a minimum stay-over period and restricted days for travel. Spouse fares are available in Europe, enabling a partner to travel half price with someone going business class. Some companies have student fares.

Provided the traveler can prove he or she is a student, the reduction can be from twenty-five to fifty percent. Youth fares in Europe for those under twenty-one are good for twenty-five percent off the standard fare. It is usually cheaper to buy a round-trip ticket, even if you don't plan on returning right away. In short, take the time to thoroughly investigate all pricing possibilities, and get quotes from at least three sources before you take out your wallet.

There are several "around the world" tickets, which sell for about $2,000, depending on how many stops you make. You usually must complete your circumnavigation of the globe in one year. The One-World alliance network, which has more than 1,000 destinations in nearly 160 countries, offers around-the-world fares that enable you to make multiple stops. Likewise, the Star Alliance Network, has 1,300 destinations in 190 countries and offers flexible deals to get you around the planet on their 28-member airlines.

As of summer 2018, the best deals to Europe by air from the United States are on WOW Air, a budget airline based in Reykjavík, Iceland that offers inexpensive tickets to travelers who do not mind giving up a few luxuries that have become standard on other airlines (bathrooms are fortunately not one of them). I flew WOW in the summer of 2017 with my family and stopped over in Iceland for a week at no extra charge. While you can certainly eat on a WOW Air flight, you'll have to pay for the luxury. You'll also have to pay for seat selections, checked bags, and oversized carry-ons.

Airline companies used to have a need to fill their planes, and thus occasionally had special fares available to sell excess seats. You could save hundreds of dollars through these deals, often offered only through email, but you needed to know about them ahead of time. Unfortunately, those days are long gone and most flights these days are overbooked. Overbooking is common practice for most airlines and is legal. As part of their business, airlines sell too many tickets with the assumption that there will be a certain percentage of "no shows"—either because people miss their flight, their previous flight is delayed, or they have a change of travel plans. According to Tanya Powley in an April 2017 article in the *Financial Times*, the statistical chance of all passengers with a valid ticket checking in on time is less than 1 in 10,000 at best.

That said, there are days with lower demand on ticket sales, which are usually midweek. Some travel websites will show you the cost of taking the same flights on alternative days in case your planning is flexible. United.com, for example, will present several alternative rates for different routes to the same destination as well as the lowest price on different days within the same week of your intended departure.

Keep in mind that the most discounted fares also have the strictest rules when it comes to refunds, changes, baggage allowances and earning frequent flyer miles or elite credit. And those of us who like to collect points will be disappointed to learn that some airlines don't award frequent flyer miles at all if you buy a ticket in the most discounted economy fare class.

Plane caveats

If I have an overnight flight, I always prefer the window seat, so I can get as much sleep as possible before I arrive. I like to put my pillow up against the window. To me there are few things as satisfying in life than falling asleep at the start of a ten-hour flight and then waking up just in time for breakfast. Before the flight takes off, I visit the bathroom, so I don't have to climb over my neighbor mid-flight. Some people prefer the aisle seat because they don't like to feel boxed in.

Be sure to double-check the flight schedule using the airline's app on your smartphone or on the airline's website. If you only have carry-on luggage, you can check-in and get your boarding pass on your phone. Check with the airline twenty-four hours in advance to make sure your departure and return times haven't changed. Sign up online for email, SMS, or smartphone alerts in case there is a last-minute change. It is always better to arrive at the airport with plenty of time to catch your flight than to miss it and have to navigate the often-expensive rebooking exercise.

Avoid flying if you can
While on the journey, I would recommend flying only if you are short of time and need to get someplace quickly, or if you need to hop over a large body of water. If the object of your trip is to visit as many places as possible in the shortest amount of time and hence you need to fly to get from A to B and from there to Z, you can save time and money by cancelling your trip and getting a subscription to National Geographic. I once met a guy at a hotel in Dili, East Timor who had arrived the night before and needed a ride the airport. I was happy to give him a ride because I was curious why his stay was so short. He said he was on limited funds and in a race to meet the criteria of the Travelers' Century Club, a nonprofit social organization representing world travelers who have visited 100 or more of the world's countries and territories. He said he needed to fly to Denpasar in Bali and connect to Bandar Seri Begawan in Brunei Darussalam, where he was spending the next night.

Flying—especially in a rush to get to some predetermined number of countries—causes you to miss out on many great opportunities. Not only that, but you miss experiencing the transition between cultures, one of the most fascinating aspects of traveling.

Flying for free

Unless you work for a travel agency or an airline, the only way to fly without paying is by getting kicked off the plane. No, really. When a plane on which you have a reserved seat is full (overbooked, the silver lining), the airline is obligated by government regulations to put you on a flight that will get you there within two hours of your original flight. If they cannot do this, they either must cut a deal with you, pay you double what your flight was worth, or pay you $400.

Airlines can oversell flights, and they frequently do, because they assume that some passengers won't show up. U.S. airlines bumped 40,000 passengers in 2017, not counting those who volunteered to give up their seats. If your changed ticket arrives at your destination between one and two hours later than planned—or between one and four hours for an international flight—the airline must pay you twice the amount of the one-way fare to your destination, up to $675. If, however, you will be delayed more than two hours— or four hours for international flights —the airline must pay you four times the one-way fare, up to $1,350. This is according to the rules and regulations of the International Air Transport Association (IATA) the trade association for the world's airlines, representing some 290 airlines or 82% of total air traffic.

If you want to take advantage of this practice, don't check a bag and be sure to check the flight's seating chart online ahead of time to see if it's sold out. To increase your chances, sit near the gate agent's desk so you can volunteer before other passengers take the offer of travel vouchers, gift cards, and sometimes cash. If offered a spot on a later flight, make sure it's a confirmed seat.

It is possible to show up for a flight that has been overbooked, and then reschedule for another flight that you think may also be overbooked. If you do this, you can get travel vouchers at both gates.

You can keep doing this as long as your luck holds out and earn enough credits to fly for the rest of the year!

Funeral discounts

To assist mourning passengers, many airlines used to offer bereavement fare discounts. More recently, airlines have begun phasing out these discounted fares. When you can find them, bereavement fares are typically open to immediate family members only. The few airlines that still offer them include Delta Air Lines, Air Canada and Lufthansa. Passengers who qualify must provide both proof of kinship and proof of death or imminent death, oftentimes including the deceased person's name, plus the name and phone number of a hospital, hospice or funeral home.

The trip in the Sudan from Wadi Halfa to Khartoum carries passengers across the Nubian Desert and some of them ride on the roof

Frequent fliers

Most airlines have systems for rewarding their patrons through bonus travel programs, but the benefits are not as generous as they used to be. You normally get points for every mile you travel with an airline, and when you collect enough, you are eligible for a free ticket.

Since American Airlines' AAdvantage program made its debut in 1981, all other airlines quickly followed suit and measured loyalty in miles. Fly 1,000 miles, earn 1,000 miles. Earn 25,000 miles and redeem them for a free domestic USA coach ticket. Earn 60,000 or so for an international round-trip ticket. Alliances then formed, with the top three being OneWorld (led by American), Star Alliance (led by United), and SkyTeam (led by Delta). I was able to accrue more than one million miles on United and was awarded with lifetime Gold status for me and a significant other.

The bad news is that these mileage-based schemes are being phased out. The loyalty programs are still there, but mileage accrual is now based on how much you spend with the airline as well as miles flown. What has also changed is the number of miles you need for a trip. Book well in advance for the tickets requiring fewer miles. On popular routes, it can be difficult to book an award ticket, and if you are able to, you may have to cash in twice as many points. So, to sum it up, you will now earn far fewer points for those economy tickets, and you will need to redeem many more of those points for free tickets.

However, it does not cost to join so even if you are just flying home for Christmas, it's wise to get on a frequent flier program. And there are still other ways to earn those points. Many credit cards work with the airlines to give you a point for every dollar charged on the cards. This is well worth considering if you use a credit card a lot, especially if you run a small business. Another way is to book your accommodation through Rocketmiles.com, where you receive from 1,000 to 5,000 miles for each night in a hotel. Be sure to compare your booking with other online sites like Expedia.com and Booking.com to make sure you are not paying too much extra for those miles. I find that Rocketmiles is a better deal in some countries than others. In New York I hardly ever use it, but in Spain it is a great deal. Compare and save and keep earning those miles.

United Airlines has a dining club that when you connect your United Airlines credit card and frequent flier account, you can earn up to five miles for every dollar spent. If you are going out with a group of friends, and are "going Dutch," offer to put the bill on your card and then collect cash from everyone for their portions of the bill.

Keeping your train of thought

Trains are a wonderful way to experience a country, and for railroad buffs, the only way. The degree of comfort and survivability will vary in different countries. In Europe, rail travel is comfortable, economical, and a good way to get around. Western Europe is the best, but standards on the other side of the now rusted Iron Curtain are quickly improving.

In Asia, Africa, and South America, riding the rails is always an adventure that will keep you writing about the experience in your journal for hours. Never will you be in want of food: At every stop each cabin is immediately transformed into an impromptu buffet as children clamber through windows and pounce through doors with bowls of every imaginable fruit and vegetable, cooked meals, and even tea or coffee.

Trains in India range from first class— the Raja form of travel that's more expensive than flying—to third class, which is like riding in a cattle car (no seats or windows; people crammed into every available space). After a twelve-hour hike through the rice paddies of Bangladesh, I arrived at a train station where the engine pulled three such cars. There was but one seat on the entire train, and when it was discovered that a foreigner was onboard, I was led directly to it. When I refused, because there were women on the train, no one would take the seat.

There's a train from Bangkok to Singapore that is in great shape and quite interesting to ride. In Peru, from Cusco to Machu Picchu, the journey by train is perhaps the most memorable in the world. And, for the mother of all rattles, there's the Trans-Siberian Railway.

The Trans-Siberian has several route possibilities, and now that the Soviet Union is history there are more chances to get off and explore along the way. Great deals on the route eastward can still

Bus trips in many lesser-developed countries have their ups and they have their downs, and some have a lot of ups and downs over very bumpy roads.

be found in Budapest. When traveling westward, check around in Hong Kong for good deals. If you wait until you get to Beijing, you may have to pay more money.

In Africa, depending on where you travel, the journey by train can be an endurance test. It also can be the only way to get to where you want to go. The trip from Dakar, Senegal to Bamako, Mali is a trip that defies imagination. The trip in the Sudan from Wadi Halfa to Khartoum carries passengers across the Nubian Desert and some of them ride on the roof (as did I). Egyptian trains are usually quite comfortable, provided you ride in second or first class, but third class is where the adventure is found. Kenya's trains are comparable to those in Europe.

Anywhere you plan to travel by train, you can usually purchase your tickets just before departure. If you are in a country with a lot of people, and especially if you are traveling anytime near a major holiday or celebration, make reservations and get your tickets ahead of time. Doing this can sometimes guarantee you a seat and assure you a more comfortable journey.

If you are planning an extensive tour of the European continent, a Eurail pass is the way to go. There are many types of passes designed to fit every schedule and budget. All passes provide unlimited travel on Europe's 100,000 miles of railroad in seventeen countries. Youth passes are available if you are under twenty-six years of age and are good for travel only in second class. Cost for the Eurail pass is anywhere from $280 for five days' travel to $680 for one month in first class, which is about twenty-five percent less for the youth pass. If you plan to travel only in Great Britain, there is the Britrail Pass. There are other similar passes available for specific European countries including the ScanRail Pass, the Swiss Travel Pass, the German Rail Pass, the Spain Rail Pass, the Benelux Pass (for Belgium, the Netherlands, and Luxembourg), the Ireland rail pass,

Austria's Rail Pass, the Italian Railway Pass, and the European East Pass for Eastern Europe.

By bus

Buses exist everywhere in the world, and you will probably find yourself traveling on them far more than any other form of transportation. Like trains, buses vary widely in their looks, construction, and degrees of comfort. While traveling across Turkey, I rode in one of the nicest buses I've seen anywhere in the world, equipped with television and free soft drinks. A twenty-eight-hour ride down Baja California in a Mexican bus was much more comfortable than many bus trips in the U.S.

Bus trips in many lesser-developed countries have their ups and they have their downs, and some have a lot of ups and downs over very bumpy roads. I have many memories of very cramped bus rides in nearly every corner of the world. The only thing I can say about these experiences is that they are a good way to meet the local people and get to know them intimately.

Buses rarely require advance ticket purchasing, but it is a good idea to ask if there is a holiday coming up when everyone and his chicken will be traveling to and from home. In most countries, there are buses between major cities on a regular basis, but there might only be one a day (or week!) to smaller outlying communities.

Buses in many countries outside the industrialized West are much different than those in Europe or North America, where all the passengers sit silently with blank looks fixated upon empty windows. To take a bus in some countries is to go to a party: Everyone is made to feel welcome. Instead of people staring at you and then glancing away quickly, they stare at you and then greet you with a warm smile when they catch your eye.

A good way to visit a new city is to play Pick and Cruise. Pick a city bus at random and sit yourself by a window, taking it to the terminus. Get on another one and ride around until you reach the end. Bring along a map and try to keep track of your location as you meander through the city streets. When you get tired of riding, get off the bus and walk back to your hotel. This is one of my favorite ways to get to know a city. I get on a bus early in the morning and ride it for about an hour and a half. Then I get off and find a small café, have breakfast, and look over my map.

After breakfast, I set out on foot and try to find my way back to where I am staying without having to look at my map again. If I think I'm lost, I just ask for directions. This way, I not only familiarize myself with the locals and their city, but I can work on my language skills and sense of orientation.

Often when you take a bus, such as in most of Africa, you will be asked to put your bags on the roof, especially if you have a large backpack. If possible, lock your bags. Make sure you take out all your valuables and put them in a daypack, keeping it securely in your lap during the trip.

Oftentimes, cargo trucks will take on paying passengers. It is not surprising to see a truck laden with tons of sacks, and then two dozen or more people hanging onto ropes on top! If you choose this form of transportation, carefully weigh all risks. Bring enough food and water for the journey.

If you have a student card be sure to present it anytime you buy a bus or train ticket, anywhere in the world. There are not always discounts, but you won't know if you don't ask. When I last visited Pakistan, students got a twenty-five percent discount on all train fares. Tourists received a twenty-five percent discount as well, just for being a foreigner. So, if you're a student and a foreigner, you can get fifty-percent off all fares!

The automobile

When traveling around a country, having your own car can offer many advantages. Volkswagen vans are both economical and are a fun way to get around. They also have the added advantage of providing a roof over your head at all times. Many travelers buy a used or new car when they get to Europe, and then sell it when they leave. If you play your cards right, you can break even or perhaps make a small profit.

The adventurous can buy a car in Europe, and drive it to West Africa or the Middle East and sell it. The route across the Sahara through Algeria, via Tamanrasset and into Niger and beyond is one of the most common routes. French cars such as the Citroën and Renault sell best in West Africa, sometimes netting a good profit. A second option, and one that is a bit more dangerous, is to buy a used Mercedes in Germany, and then drive through Austria, Slovenia, Croatia, Montenegro, Greece, and Turkey and sell it in Syria or Lebanon. If you can get it there without any bullet holes you should be able to double or even triple your investment. The third route is through Turkey, Iran, and Pakistan, and into India and Nepal. From what I hear, large trucks and buses are in demand in these regions.

From the United States, the most common vehicle travel is into Mexico or Canada. Some venture beyond. In Mexico, it is getting increasingly easier to travel by one's own car as gas stations open up throughout rural areas and campgrounds are established. Traveling in Mexico by car is almost as hassle-free as it is in the States. Perhaps the best car to bring into Mexico is the Volkswagen because many of them are manufactured there. If one breaks down on you, it is easy to find parts and a mechanic who is familiar with your engine. Also, since many people in Mexico drive VWs, if you drive one—especially a beaten up dilapidated one, you are less likely to be accosted for special fees at police checkpoints.

If you drive further south than Mexico and plan to drive into Guatemala and Honduras, the rules are like elsewhere in the lesser-developed parts of the world. Bringing your own vehicle into countries outside the industrialized world can have both advantages and disadvantages. It gives you increased flexibility for getting to remote places, but it sets you up as a wealthy tourist and hence a target for theft. There are additional hassles at border crossings, where you must have all the proper insurance, an international driver's license, and a carnet to prove that you won't sell the vehicle in their country.

Be sure to have the proper insurance before driving into another country. This rule holds especially true for Mexico. Do not assume that your insurance back home will cover you, because it will not. In Mexico, if you are in an accident, and do not have Mexican insurance, you could go to jail and may stay there for several days or even weeks.

It is also a good idea to get insurance that covers the loss of your vehicle. If your vehicle breaks down in the middle of nowhere and you must fly home, the cost of insurance will be far less than the fines you must pay a foreign government for leaving a car there.

Renting a car

I have rented cars in countries as diverse as Thailand, Tunisia, Brazil and South Africa. In Helsinki I rented a small car with unlimited mileage and drove it all the way up to Nordkap and back – more than 3,000 kilometers in a week. Needless to say, the folks at Avis were not pleased with me when I returned. Good thing the car had the unlimited mileage option.

Renting a car can give you freedom and flexibility when you're traveling, and in some parts of the world it's really the best way to get around. There are many options in terms of rental companies and the types of cars available. If you're traveling with children or with a lot of gear, you may want a large SUV. If you're simply looking to save money on rental rates and gas, you'll want to reserve the smallest available model – and perhaps even a hybrid that gets 40 miles to the gallon. Be sure to check that the mileage is unlimited – so you don't get an unwelcome surprise when you return the car.

You'll find major international car rental agencies all over the world — such as Alamo, Avis, Budget, Dollar, Enterprise, Hertz, National, Sixt, and Thrifty. But depending on where you're traveling, locally owned companies could offer lower rates, but before booking, read reviews as there are a lot of scammers and charlatans who may not be very honest. For this reason, I usually go with the brands I trust, such as Hertz. I compare prices on Expedia.com and the website of the companies themselves. You may also want to try booking using hotwire.com, a service that gives you first the price, and then after you pay they provide the name of the company from which you will be renting.

You must decide how to insure your rental car. I have a credit card that includes auto insurance when I use that card to pay for the rental. It only works when you decline ALL OTHER insurance from the rental company. It works quite well, even when the accident is your fault. Otherwise you will want to go with the insurance the rental company offers you. In no circumstances whatsoever should you drive without insurance.

No matter which company you choose, be sure to hang onto all your paperwork (including the checklist used by the company to check the car's condition when you turn it in) for a few months after the rental period, in case a billing dispute arises.

If you do rent a car, I suggest bringing with you three essential items: 1) a smart phone to use as a GPS; 2) a lighter socket USB charger; and 3) a dashboard mount to hold your phone so that you can see the screen while driving. Avoid getting the windshield mount because the suction cups don't stay on very well -- and the last thing you want is for your phone to crash onto the dash when you make a sharp turn or hit a bump. When you return the rental car, the same advice applies as when you check out of a hotel room: check everywhere carefully for your belongings, even if you are sure you have not forgotten anything. If there is more than one of you, have everyone check. If you have kids, give them a reward if they find something.

Motorcycles

Emilio Scotto left Argentina with a Honda Goldwing and $300 in 1985. Eight years and 10,000 gallons of gas later, he had circumnavigated the earth, and visited 142 countries. The 285,000-mile Odyssey landed him in Los Angeles, where he planned to go back around the planet the other way, because he missed forty-three countries. His goal was to visit every country in the world on his motorcycle within ten years.

Jim Rogers chose a BMW motorbike as his vehicle of choice and spent twenty-two months traveling 160,000 kilometers across six continents, exploring investment opportunities along the way. Jim started his journey from Ireland, crossed Europe and rode through various Central Asian Republics before entering China from the west and crossing the Taklamakan desert to reach Beijing. He flew to Tokyo and went on to cross Russia from east to west, across Siberia. After arriving back in Ireland, he set off on the next and the tougher stretch: South across the Sahara Desert and through Africa from Tunisia to South Africa. From South Africa he headed off to Australia and New Zealand, then across to South and Central America where he had to cross through countries with active civil wars like Peru, Guatemala, and El Salvador.

Neil Walker was a colleague of mine at the United Nations who left for his duty station in Kyrgyzstan while I was leaving to work in Geneva. We both departed New York with our most prized forms of transport—he on his BMW and me on my Harley (flying them to our respective destinations). He was later posted in Kiev and drove out twice to Geneva from the Ukraine on his Beemer.

Motorcycles have wonderful advantages and are considered the only mode of transportation by many die-hard bikers. Motorbikes allow you to experience the elements, feeling at one with the country and its nature. They, like bicycles, are a good conversation piece and an easy way to meet people. Motorcycles cover greater distances than bicycles, and get you there with more energy to spare

While based in Europe with the UN, I discovered a way to explore the continent without taking too much time off work. I started with a weekend ride to Munich, where I left my Harley at the airport and flew back early Monday morning on easyJet, a low-cost budget airline with flights for about 50 euro. Friday evening, I flew back and picked up the bike and drove south to Croatia, where I left the bike at a Harley shop in Split (for servicing) on Monday morning and flew back to Geneva. The following weekend I made it down to Montenegro, the weekend after that through Albania to Brindisi, Italy (by ferry), and the weekend after that from Brindisi to Sicily. After exploring Sicily (where there are three easyJet cities with cheap flights to Geneva) I took a ferry to Sardinia (where there are another three easyJet cities), from there another ferry to Corsica (with another three airports), then finally a ferry from Bastia in the north of Corsica to Toulon, in the South of France.

If you plan to travel by motorcycle, look for something in the 750cc range. This will give you enough power to carry gear and get to where you want to go but it is light enough to dodge potholes and chickens. Wear lots of protective clothing, including a helmet. Always carry a spare key. Hide your spare somewhere on your bike using a Zip Tie or duct tape, or trade keys with a traveling companion (or leave it someplace with someone who could send it via DHL or FedEx if needed). Keep your stuff dry in saddlebags by using trash compactor bags.

Motorcycles have wonderful advantages and are considered the only mode of transportation by many die-hard bikers.

When traveling by motorcycle, it is a good idea to have a sleeping bag, a small stove, and plenty of provisions. Carry enough tools to make minor repairs. The foam-in-a-can tire repair is a must. If you're traveling into an area without many garages, bring spare spark plugs and minor parts. Be especially careful when traveling by motorbike; one small accident can ruin an otherwise enjoyable journey.

Rules of thumb

Hitchhiking is not for everybody, but if you do choose to hitch rides when traveling, there are a few rules of thumb to keep in mind.

Never think that you need to take the first ride. Trust your instinct, and if you have any doubts about the car that has stopped to pick you up, turn it down. Hitchhiking does entail risks, but it is safer in most parts of the world than in the United States.

Women traveling alone should be especially careful when choosing the ride they want to accept. Men traveling alone have fewer problems but have fewer cars stop for them because of the obvious risk drivers are considering. By far the hitchhikers who travel quickest are those who travel as a couple.

When you do get a lift, remember that you are a guest in someone else's home. Make that person glad he or she picked you up. Ask a lot of questions, and keep the person involved in conversation. This is a good opportunity to get firsthand information on the region. Always be willing to give something in return for the lift, be it an impromptu English lesson, great conversation, or just keeping the driver awake on a long drive.

To get that ride when it comes your way, you must be ready. You have perhaps five seconds to project your personality and convince the driver that giving you a lift will be the best thing he or she has done all day. Dress appropriately and wear a big smile. It makes one wonder to see hikers on the side of the road dressed in last month's laundry and carrying a bad attitude all over their face. They look like they've been standing there a week, and it's easy to see why.

When hitching in crowded areas, like trying to leave a college town in Europe, be original—there's a lot of competition. Keep smiling, and wave to the cars that drive by. Once when hitching to Monaco from Aix-en-Provence in the south of France, I was about to be passed by two young women in a sports car. I went down on my knees, clasping my hands together in supplication. The women burst out laughing as their car came screeching to a stop.

When hitching, stand at a point in the road where it is long and straight, and the traffic is moving relatively slow. Gas stations, border stations, traffic lights, restaurants, truck stops, and rest areas are all excellent places to score a lift. If the sun has set, and you want to continue hitching, make sure the place is well lit and that there is no danger of getting run over.

If you find yourself stuck beside the road when night falls, don't fret. If you are far from habitation, look for something with a roof, such as an abandoned building or the like. Make yourself comfortable and get some rest.

If you are near a town, ask the locals where you might find a bed that you could reserve for the night. If you have a tent, ask if you can pitch it in their yard. You will probably be turned down for any offer of payment, but it's best to get it settled up front.

Hitching is only common in the West, though I have had remarkable experiences thumbing around the Middle East, and in parts of Asia, Africa, and Central America.

When hitching outside of Europe or the U.S., keep in mind that the "thumbs-up" gesture is not universally recognized. In fact, it can be downright insulting in many parts of the world. When in doubt, hold your hand out and casually point at the road with your index figure. This gets the message across, and is not likely to offend anyone.

There are likely to be more hitchhikers in Europe, America, and Australia than in other parts of the world. While traveling in these areas, you will often arrive at your "hitching post" to find several hikers already waiting for lifts there. The unwritten rule is that new arrivals move further down the road.

A sign indicating your direction or destination is very helpful. Don't advertise a destination that is far away: Every little bit helps, and if the driver is going all the way he may not want to make an immediate decision about taking someone he has yet to meet. Write the name of the place in the local language: München instead of Munich, l'allemagne if traveling to Germany from France or Deutschland if traveling from Austria.

Bicycles

I have met many travelers on bikes around the world, and even a couple on a bicycle built for two peddling across the Sahara. Some were really enjoying themselves, others were in excruciating pain. Europe is probably the best destination if you plan to travel by bicycle, especially in Holland where there are bike paths everywhere and it's not very far between towns.

Nadine Slavinski, in her book, *Cycling Europe: Budget Bike Touring in the Old World*, says that cycling is, "…an extremely personal, up-close way to travel. The energy you put into getting yourself, your bicycle, and your gear from point to point is immediately rewarded with concrete results. You are constantly greeted by new surroundings and can take pride in looking back and knowing that you met the challenge of the terrain and distance that day."

She also states that traveling by bicycle "brings you closer to the land you are touring as well as its people, who have a greater respect for you as a cyclist than they would as an ordinary tourist."

If you choose to travel by bike, be sure to bring lots of spare parts and containers for water. Bicycles are relatively inexpensive and easily repaired. Because they are a humble form of transportation, bicycles can help you to make friends in any country and in any language. They can be carried on planes, on trains, on boats, and buses. You can even take your bike into your hotel room and sleep with it if you wish. I can't say that about traveling on a Harley.

If you are planning a major bike trip around the world, start with one around your neighborhood first. Then take a few full-day trips, then some weekend rides. Be sure you are in excellent shape and are aware of just what you are getting yourself into. When in good shape, you should be able to average sixty to eighty miles a day on a bicycle.

Mountain bikes are usually much heavier than road bikes and a lot slower. They are, however, great for getting "off the beaten track" and for exploring trails. When you want to get off the road and look for a place to camp, nothing beats a mountain bike.

Bikes are a great way to get around cities, especially in India where you can rent them at very reasonable prices. In most parts of the world you can rent a bicycle by the hour or by the day. This is a good way to see the sights, or simply to get around, if you are going to be there for a while. In many cities in Europe and North America, you can rent bikes with credit cards at automatic stations. Citi Bike, for example, is a privately-owned public bicycle sharing system with 706 stations and 12,000 bikes serving New York City and Jersey City, New Jersey. In Geneva,

Switzerland, Genève roule is a nonprofit public-benefit association with a dual objective: Promote cycling and "socio-occupational integration."

If you're planning a long stint in a country, consider buying a bike instead of renting it for a long time. You should be able to sell it when you leave. Chinese bikes are heavy and sturdy and available just about everywhere around Africa and Asia. In Europe, check the classified ads and the bulletin boards at youth hostels.

Boats

Traveling by boat is one of the most enjoyable, therapeutic, and peaceful forms of transportation available. Whether you are barging

The most common form of water travel (for travelers) is paying passage on a ferry or passenger liner.

up a river, sailing across an ocean, or kayaking through a fjord, the tranquility of the water makes it one of the best joys of motion.

The most common form of water travel (for travelers) is paying passage on a ferry or passenger liner. Cruises are nice, but don't usually qualify for mention in a book on experiential travel. However, one exception may be the transatlantic crossing on the seven-day voyage on the Queen Mary 2. The company insists it is not a transatlantic cruise, but an "Atlantic crossing." For those people who abhor jet travel, this is the ideal way to travel between North America (New York) and Europe (Southampton or Hamburg). Sailing into the United States on a ship, passing the Statue of Liberty at sunrise is a memorable experience. I took the ship on the 100th anniversary of the sinking of the Titanic.

When visiting the Greek Islands, you will probably travel by boat. There is a boat that offers passage from Greece to Haifa in Israel, and sometimes to Alexandria in Egypt. Ferries ply the English Channel regularly from Dover to Calais and to other ports on the European continent. In Mexico, you can travel to various points on the Baja peninsula to the mainland. One of my favorites in the United States is from Bellingham, Washington, north to Skagway, Alaska.

Traveling on boats is pretty much like traveling by train: You buy a ticket and go. If you are a couple and want privacy, you can get a berth. Otherwise, there is always a place to roll out a sleeping bag if the trip lasts longer than a day.

River travel is more interesting than ocean travel because the scenery is more varied. Wherever there is a large river anywhere in the world, there is some form of public transportation. Bangladesh has more navigable rivers than drivable roads. Zaire keeps its country together through river travel. The Gambia exists because of its river with the country's boundaries stretching along the river's path.

Many of the towns and villages along the Amazon are only accessible by riverboat.

The range of comfort in river travel ranges from floating hotels on the Nile to barges on the Congo. My longest and most memorable river trip was on the Upper Nile from Kosti to Juba in the Sudan, a journey of 1,500 miles. The craft was a rigged collection of six decrepit barges, tied together with metal cord and pushed from behind by a tugboat.

The journey took fourteen days. There were 3,000 people, a few hundred animals, and two foreigners. The journey, though long, took me right into the heart of Africa. I experienced, in slow motion, the gradual transition from Sahara Desert through savannah to tropical jungle, and from Arab culture to that of the African south.

In the Gambia, the river journey from Banjul to Basse Santa Su lasts two days and takes you past the village where the story behind the epic film, *Roots*, originated.

In South America, you can travel from the headwaters of the Amazon in Peru through Iquitos and down to Tabatinga on the border with Brazil, and then eventually all the way to Belém on the Atlantic Coast. Most of the rivercraft are slow-going boats in which you string up your hammock and curl up with a good book. Between some segments of the 4,000-mile journey, speed boats are available, which are appropriately called *rapidos*. I took one from Iquitos to Manaus once where they even served sandwiches and drinks. The long boat had a Chevy 351 engine mounted on a pedestal and with a propeller mounted on the far end of the drive shaft.

If you take a riverboat, try to get on it as early as possible, especially if you are in a heavily populated country like Bangladesh or Brazil. Stake out a piece of territory on the boat and don't leave it unless you're traveling companion (if you have one) can stand guard over your possessions. If you are on a journey that is going to last several days or weeks, don't pitch your camp near the bathrooms, for obvious reasons. In the rainy seasons, make sure you have cover if you are on a barge.

As with any form of long-distance travel, when traveling by boat, carry provisions with you. There is usually a small cafeteria on most boats, but don't rely on it. Make sure you ask before what, if any, amenities there will be. Have enough water (or purification tablets to sanitize the boat's water), some fruit, nuts, crackers—whatever you can find to eat on the way.

If you are in the tropics, don't forget your mosquito repellent. The lights on the boat attract a lot of bugs, and if you are sleeping out in the open you could be considered an open buffet for them.

If there is no public transport going where you want to travel, you can usually find a private boat that will take you. The possibilities range from hiring a falouka in Egypt to travel down the Nile, to paying a fisherman for the use of his boat on the Ganges in India.

If you do opt for this private option, check the boat thoroughly before leaving to make sure you won't spring a leak and be stuck up the creek, so to speak. This happened to me on the Nile: Some friends and I hired a falouka with a captain to carry us from Aswan to Luxor. An hour into the trip the boat started to take on water through several holes in the hull. We all pitched in and paddled like crazy to get to the nearest shore.

Getting on a yacht or sailing vessel to cross oceans is a dream of many travelers. Put up a notice at a local yacht club, which exist throughout the world. The chances of getting a response are slim if you have no previous sailing experience, but even so it is always worth a try. I didn't have any experience prior to looking for a sailboat in the Philippines, but I put a notice up at the yacht club in Manila and got a response. A month later I had plenty of experience, although the German captain was not too thrilled when he discovered I did not know my starboard from portside.

If you live in a port city like San Diego, it may be a good idea to get some training before your departure, especially if you plan on doing a lot of island hopping around the Caribbean or South Pacific. Get certified as a scuba diver, too. The more experience you have on and in the water, the easier it will be to get rides.

Travel on freighters is exciting, but unfortunately the days are long gone when you could ask around a wharf and get a lift in exchange for work. Tight regulations by the International Seamen's Union make it impossible for a cargo ship to even take you on.

If there is no public transport going where you want to travel, you can usually find a private boat that will take you.

The best chance of traveling by freighter is to go as a paying passenger. An increasing number of cargo companies are offering this service to bring in extra income. It is not cheap, with an average daily cost of around $150 a day for room and board. Because of the cost, the people who usually take advantage of cargo travel are retired folks who have the wherewithal to go.

For all things cruising, including paying fare on freighters, I recommend The Cruise People Ltd at www.cruisepeople.co.uk/.

To walk a mile for a camel

In different parts of the world you will come across the opportunity to travel on the back of a horse, a camel, or even an elephant. The experience ranges from a tourist ride to a full-scale excursion. In the Indian state of Rajasthan, you can hire a camel for several days and journey out into the desert. I once went for a week, sleeping out under the stars, cooking curry over a fire, and acquainting myself with the rhythms of the desert. I visited many rural villages that are only accessible by this ancient mode of transportation. When Mohammed (my guide) and I would ride into a village, the entire population would run out to greet us. In the lowlands of Nepal, I spent a day in the forest on the back of an elephant looking for a rhinoceros. We found him at nightfall.

If you plan to stay for a while in a place where you can do this, I would highly recommend traveling somewhere by the way of the nomads—on the back of a camel, horse, or elephant. While out in the desert or the mountains, you'll be able to experience an ancient way of life many people think only exists in legends and history books.

9:

Traveling Companions

"The man who travels alone can start today; but he who travels with another must wait till that other is ready."

— *Henry David Thoreau*

Both traveling alone and with someone carry advantages: Freedom is great, but it is always nice to be able to share the beauty of a sunset with a friend.

In this chapter I will look at the pros and cons of traveling alone, traveling as a couple, traveling with children, traveling with friends, and traveling with strangers.

Traveling alone

There are many advantages to traveling alone including the ability to meet and interact with local people. When you travel with someone, your attention is often focused on that person and on speaking the language you share with that person. When you are alone, you are more apt to reach out to people for human contact, conversation, and company. Likewise, when you are alone, locals are more likely to approach you.

As Thoreau said, traveling alone also brings the freedom to go where you want, when you want, and how you want. Both traveling alone and with someone carry advantages: Freedom is great, but it is always nice to be able to share the beauty of a sunset with a friend.

Having your cake and eating it too
When you travel alone, it is usually not very difficult to meet a friend with whom you can share the sunset and then go back to

traveling alone after a few sunsets. However, if you start your journey with someone and then opt for the alone option mid-way, it may be difficult to reconcile that with the other person.

You will constantly meet new friends on the road with whom you will be able to travel for short or extended periods of time. Many of these people you will probably remain in touch with for the rest of your life.

For me a very important part of traveling, as opposed to touring, is gaining access to the "inside" of a country; connecting with its

A very important part of traveling is gaining access to the "inside" of a country; connecting with its people and experiencing human interaction.

people and experiencing human interaction, if only for a moment, that confirms you are a fellow human on this rock called Earth and not just another foreigner passing through. It is becoming easier and easier to travel to faraway places but remain outsiders there always, separated by the same distance of consciousness even though geographically you may be in the same room.

While traveling alone has its advantages, and I would recommend it to anyone seeking the ultimate travel experience, I would be remiss if I were to say it is the only way to travel. If I had not traveled with a partner or traveled with children I would not have had the full travel experience because traveling as a couple and traveling with children can open up opportunities unimagined by the solo traveler. Thus, to really gain that ultimate travel experience in a country, you would need to experience it as a solo traveler, as a couple, and with children. In fact, the same country visited in each of these three ways could be like visiting three different countries because of the different experiences one would have through each. In other words, for example, the local experiences you will encounger when traveling with kids will be much different that when traveling alone or as a couple.

Travel as a couple

If you are traveling abroad with someone with whom you have a friendship or relationship, make sure you know that person really well and that your "ship" is sea-worthy. Traveling can put a lot of stress on a relationship and many couples and friends do not make it through the travel experience together.

Especially as a couple, both of you will go through many changes and your senses will awaken to many new experiences. It is wonderful to be able to grow through this experience with someone, but this is rarely the case. I know of some couples who travel abroad with romantic notions of shared experiences and end up breaking up while on the road.

Traveling with a companion also is a good way to test the waters with someone you may be pondering distant horizons with. Before popping the big question, consider an adventurous travel adventure with your significant other. Traveling, in many ways, can push your partner away from his or her comfort zones, which will let you discover his or her positive and negative traits (I find that everyone has both).

Also, the combination of culture shock and exhausting globe-trotting can somehow bring out some of the deeply hidden flaws of your partner's character. That's why you should notice how your loved one acts toward hotel staff, flight attendants, and waiters during your time together on the road—as there is no better method of judging someone's character.

Discuss all expectations for the trip before the trip

Both of you may have agreed on a destination but you might have very different ideas of what to do once you arrive. One may dream of a romantic getaway while the other envisages more adventurous pursuits like scuba diving, rock climbing, or hiking. One may have prepared a super detailed itinerary while the other may prefer to meander and remain spontaneous. Be sure to talk through your preferences and draft up a list of activities and experiences you both agree on before embarking on your journey.

Give each other space

Even hanging out with Mother Teresa or the Dalai Lama 24/7 is bound to create tensions at some point. As much as you may love someone, organize time to chill out alone—or pursue those things the other does not care much about like scuba diving, rock climbing, or hiking. One can go shopping while the other hangs in a tavern. Go scuba diving while your partner reads on the beach. Book some things to do together, but be sure to explore things on your own, and share stories when you are back together in the evening. This approach is particularly useful if one likes to sleep in the morning while the other is an early riser.

Don't let the money get you down
If you are sharing expenses, be sure to discuss the budget in advance and work out who will pay for what. Don't let disagreements over finances ruin your time together. Long before we were married my wife and I would each contribute $500 a month into a joint travel fund, which we would then use for traveling excursions—often last-minute weekend warrior outings all over the world from Buenos Aries to Tokyo.

Avoid getting hangry
Tempers often run high when one (or both) of you are hungry. Curb hunger (and anger) by discussing approximate meal times for the day before you head out into the world, and always carry snacks. Make sure that you clearly communicate when you're hungry and reaching your breaking point.

While traveling with a significant other can be difficult, it can also be extremely rewarding. You can see the world together and share experiences that will enrich your lives for years to come. Traveling as a couple is a great way to meet local couples and gain insights that would otherwise be inaccessible as a solo traveler. Traveling with a partner can also help you deal with underlying issues in both personalities, and thus test your relationship and help you develop stronger ties to one another (rather than if you had just stayed at home in your comfort zone).

Traveling with friends

To travel is to embrace the amazing. Traveling with friends can be even more amazing—at times. Friends can either augment the quality of travel, or they can ruin it, making you wish you'd gone alone.

To help make the best of a travel experience with friends, and to avoid wishing you had done it alone, first be clear about what everyone wants. Just because you all want to go to Bali doesn't mean you all expect to do the same things. You may be thinking ninety percent beaches and ten percent temples, and they're thinking the opposite. If this is not settled before you board the plane, there will be a risk of conflict.

And remember, just because you are traveling together doesn't mean you must do everything together. In fact, the best groups I've traveled with often did do things separately. Not every day, but every few days. It made for lively conversation at dinner as each shared their experiences. This is the same for traveling as a couple. Everyone needs some "me" time, especially introverts traveling in a group. It's not being anti-social—it's just some quiet time (or music-infused time) to recharge the social batteries.

The second thing to keep in mind is thinking about how everyone prefers to travel. I love budget hotels and am perfectly content walking and taking public transport. However, I have friends who prefer cars with drivers, fifty pounds of luggage, and five-star hotels. *Chaque un son gout*, as the French say: "To each his own."

When traveling with friends, money can be a source of tension if you are not careful. If you let yourself fixate on a few dollars here and there it could ruin your trip. If it becomes a big enough deal to ruin the trip, then you may want to consider politely going off on your own.

To avoid tense scenarios, manage expectations ahead of time. Chances are someone makes less than everyone else and is not looking forward to splitting a $400 meal four ways when all they had was a salad. Discussing it ahead of time may give an embarrassed travel companion the chance to talk about it separately from the group.

As with all travel advice—or life advice for that matter—try not to make *any* decisions when hungry or stressed. Most people get cranky when they're hungry. Throw in the stress of transit to the mix (getting to an airport, missing a train, etc.) and together these are bad times to have a serious conversation.

That said, as in all things group-oriented from travel to the work place, communication is key. Group dynamics are fickle and delicate. Don't let tensions or misunderstandings build up and fester. I've seen this happen and it's toxic. A presumed slight, a mistake on a check, any number of things can build into a big issue. Be direct with an open heart if you sense anything that may cause discomfort. Dealing with tense moments in the moment may bring laughter whereas ignoring them and letting them build up unintentionally could bring disaster, distracting everyone from the purpose of the trip, which is to experience a country together and learn from what it has to offer.

10:

Traveling with Children

"Look at the world with the child's eye
—it is very beautiful."

– *Kailash Satyarthi*

Kids have an unadulterated, sincere, and curious view of the world that many adults have lost.

Traveling with children can introduce an entirely new and refreshing dimension to the travel experience. As a solo/independent traveler in my teens and early twenties I would never have considered the thought of group travel with little ones. However, having travelled with my kids on numerous occasions, I can honestly say that I can recommend it whole-heartedly.

Kids have an unadulterated, sincere, and curious view of the world that many adults have lost. When you are traveling with children you will undoubtedly get swept up in their authenticity, vulnerability, laughter, tears, and pure joy. If we, as adults, can incorporate some of these child-like perspectives into our journeys, we can learn to live more from the heart. When the heart softens we can more truly feel, connect, and understand the joy the world has to offer.

Before the trip

If you're traveling with kids, planning is key. The following are a few caveats to keep in mind, based on my own experiences and supplemented by a list from the United States Transportation Security Administration's (TSA) website to help you make the journey with minimal risk and headache.

Most destinations these days have webpages with lists of things you can do with kids. For example, www.bangkok.com/kids.htm has a lot of suggestions of things to do with your kids in the Thai capital. If heading to South Africa, www.capetownmagazine.com/to-do-kids should be your first stop online.

Once you've researched your destination, prepare a list of possible activities that take various lengths of time and suit different weather conditions. If you've more than one child, let both or all choose different things to do from the list.

Keep a journal with your kids and encourage them to draw and list things they see and eat. Encourage them to learn new words in the local languages, and list them in the journal. They could also collect autographs and doodles from people they meet as well as ticket stubs and candy wrappers. Paste in maps and get the children to highlight or circle the places you've seen.

Before you get to the airport, explain the security routine to kids. Especially if your kids will be flying for the first time, tell them in advance what to expect during the security screening process. If your kids love to pull practical jokes, be sure to let them know beforehand that "my dad has a bomb" jokes are unacceptable.

Know before you go

Prepare a few holiday-related projects before you leave to prepare the kiddos for what's to come. A few ideas include exploring maps, reading books together, or watching shows on the history, geography, animal, and plant life of your destination. Try visiting restaurants for the destination and trying some new foods; if going to Thailand, for example, go to a Thai restaurant and introduce your kids to pad thai.

Take your time and plan for a slower pace than you might be used to when traveling alone or as a couple. My usual advice throughout this book is to plan to see less to enable you to see more—and this holds doubly true when you have young ones with you. The less you feel you must pack in, the more enjoyable and stress-free your travel will be. If you plan on walking or cycling, remember that young children won't want to focus on getting from A to B, but on following their own interests so allow time for exploring. This is something that you can learn from them. The journey is usually much more interesting than the destination.

Consider travelling with another family and sharing the responsibilities. Before you go, discuss what each person wants to do and agree on how to share time hanging out with the kids, spending time together as families and apart on "date nights."

If any of your kids has a serious allergy, travel with a card that specifies, in the language of your destination, what they're allergic to and how serious the condition is. Allergy UK produces cards in twenty-seven different languages (allergyuk.org).

Booking accommodation

Consider a home exchange with another family that has kids the same age(s) as yours. If you connect with another family you can end up with a child-proofed home, toys to play with, and insider information on things to do with kids as well as access to healthcare services. I have used homeexchange.com, but others include homelink.org and matchinghouses.com (house swaps for families with special needs). You may also want to consider farm stays and university accommodations (venuemasters.co.uk); these have potential family advantages such as animals to look at, sports facilities, and wide-open spaces.

If you are planning to stay in hotels, be sure to let them know ahead of time how many beds you will need. Some hotels have family discounts. When you arrive, check the room thoroughly for safety issues, such as guard rails on the balcony, sharp edges on the furniture, etc. Don't hesitate to change the room if you are not comfortable with the first one given.

Preparation

Visas: If your destination requires a visa (see Chapter 15 on Red Tape), don't be surprised if the fee for the kids is the same as for yours. As many countries require visas to be collected in person by applicants (including children), you and the kids may have to make a trip to the embassies together.

More red tape: In most cases you will need much more documentation for the kids than for yourself—especially if you have an adopted child, are traveling without the child's other parent, or if one of you has a different name from the child. Remember, when it comes to red tape it is better to have and not need than to need and not have. If the child is adopted you must take their adoption papers; and if you're the only parent travelling—regardless of your marital status—you will need proof of consent from the other parent for your child to travel with you, especially when in countries where overseas adoption and/or child trafficking is common. If the name on your child's passport is not the same as yours, or if your child bears little resemblance to you, you will probably be asked at immigration to show proof of parentage. The standard doc kit should include your child's birth certificate, your marriage certificate (if applicable), and a signed and attested consent letter from the other parent confirming you can travel with your child. If the other parent is no longer alive, bring the death certificate, just in case.

See your doctor at least two months before you leave to discuss your travel plans. Bring everyone's vaccination records, and ask the doctor to note down their blood groups for you. If any of your children has a pre-existing medical condition, it may be a good idea to ask for help in identifying a doctor in your destination who specializes in the same condition.

Stock up on non-prescription antihistamine pills such as Piriton for symptoms such as sneezing, streaming noses, or itchy eyes. For skin allergies, try applying over-the-counter Hydrocortisone cream.

If malaria is present in any of the places you plan to visit (check the list of affected countries at who.int/ith/en), get appropriate specialist advice on the appropriate antimalarial medication and dosage for children. You'll also need to make sure you take ample supplies of insect repellent, clothes to cover everyone up in the evenings, and bed-nets infused with insecticide (don't worry, they are safe for kids). You can get antimalarial medicine in syrup form for kids though tablets are much more common. As children are usually prescribed smaller amounts of the same antimalarials as adults, you may need to break the pills up into pieces.

Air travel with kids

I think the iPad is the greatest invention for entertaining kids since the rattle. Be sure to load up on appropriate movies before you leave. iPads can also be extremely useful on road trips in a car or bus. Be sure to bring headphones. However, a caveat: Recent research is showing links between excessive screen-time and obesity, sleep disorders, aggression, poor social skills, depression, and academic underachievement. So, while the iPad can bring temporary engagement and can be used for good (i.e. watching documentaries about your destination or learning the language en route), they should not be used excessively and seen as a panacean pacifier.

For toddlers, be sure to pack playing cards, small toys, books, games like chess, and coloring books in your bag. Once on board, don't whip them all out at once or let him rummage through. Take them out one at a time and let her play with each until she's really ready to move on to the next distraction. You may want to leave those noisy toys at home, unless you want to unsettle a plane full of fellow travelers.

Always ask about available seats. If you didn't purchase a seat for your toddler (kids under two years old can sit on your lap), expect a full flight and know your chances of getting one are slim. But ask anyway. Many airlines now let you check in online, which allows you to book preferred seats from home and avoid the long lines at check-in. If you have one child under two, you can book your seats on line using the seating chart: book the window and aisle and hope the middle seat stays empty.

Don't forget to take advantage of early boarding. When they make the call for travelers who need extra time to board, that is your call. Use the time to stash bags where you want them before the overhead bins fill up.

Pack as much baby food, breast milk, and formula that you may need. If you're traveling with a baby or toddler, don't worry about the three-ounce container rule—just travel with as much food as needed to reach your destination.

Bring snacks for older kids. Many flights (even lengthy ones) no longer offer in-flight food service. There's nothing worse than being on a plane with a bunch of hangry (hungry+angry) kids.

Double-check the flight schedule. While you always want to arrive at the airport with plenty of time to catch your flight (leaving extra time for unpredictable kid mishaps), you won't want to spend the night at the airport if you can avoid it.

Print your boarding passes at home. Airlines offer this time-saving feature on their websites—and it means you won't have to occupy the kids while everyone snakes back and forth in line to check in at the airport. You can also use the e-check in kiosks when you arrive. It's not as fast as having boarding passes in hand, but still better than the line.

If you are traveling alone with the kids, consider the "meet and assist" services when booking your flight. This is generally provided by the airport and not the airline and depends for the most part on

Traveling with children can introduce an entirely new and refreshing dimension to the travel experience.

the availability of staff, but if you're traveling as a single parent with more than one child, you'll be given priority.

Prepare for takeoff and landing. Get your kids to drink a lot of water on the flight. The low humidity of cabin air can cause mild dehydration as well as dry and irritated nostrils. When ascending or descending the change in air pressure can cause air expansion in the middle ear and sinuses, which can be painful for babies and infants because of their smaller ear passages. Chewing gum usually helps, as does breast-feeding or drinking from a bottle. If any of these are not possible, massage your child's ears from behind and give the earlobes a few gentle tugs from time to time. Force yourself to yawn—the mere act of yawning can cause others to yawn. Swallowing or yawning opens the Eustachian tube and allows air to flow into or out of the middle ear. This helps equalize pressure on either side of the ear drum, thus alleviating the discomfort. Another trick that often works for me, and which I learned from scuba diving, is pinching my nose and closing my mouth, and then trying to blow hard through my nose.

Keeping your kids healthy and safe

Stay together. If you will be in relatively crowded places, such as the Grand Bazaar of Marrakesh, don't forget to designate a meeting point in case anyone gets separated from the family. Tell your kids the importance of staying together, but don't scare them. I would always bring walkie-talkies for everyone—you can usually get packs of four walkie-talkies online or in most electronic stores. Child monitors can also be a real help to keep an eye on young children in crowded places such as airports and shopping malls. The parent carries a tracking device about the size of a TV remote control while the child wears a watch-like contraption. If the child moves beyond a pre-set distance, or if the bracelet is removed, an alarm sounds. Once the tracker sounds the alarm, you can push a button to set off a beeper on your child's bracelet to help you track him or her down.

Stay sane and sanitize. Carry a bottle of hand sanitizer with you always, both for yourself and for the kids. Rub it carefully over your hands and fingers before every meal.

Whether for the heat or cold, bring clothes made from natural fibers. Sweat irritates delicate skin and can lead to prickly heat or sweat rash. Children will need two sets of clothes per day as well as sunhats with wide brims and neck flaps when playing outdoors. Get good sunglasses (or goggles with elasticated straps, which stay on better) with UV protection as children's eyes are highly vulnerable to glare.

Watch the water. If the tap water isn't safe to drink, you'll need to boil, filter, or sterilize your own, or buy bottled water. Make sure the children don't drink from the sink, even when brushing teeth. You may need to supervise them. An ounce of prevention is better than a pound of cure. Always keep a bottle of drinking water by the sink as a helpful reminder.

Avoid the buffets. They're a dwelling ground for the bugs that cause diarrhea. Instead, eat at busy places where the turnover of food is fast. If the cutlery is wet, giving it a dry wipe with a clean tissue to reduce the risk of bacteria. Check that bottles and cans are unopened before handing these to children (and then use straws—do not let them drink from the bottle or can). In some countries, it may be advisable to avoid ice and salads.

11:

Accommodation

"All saints can do miracles,
but few of them can keep a hotel."

— *Mark Twain*

To ensure you a bed at the end of the day, and one that is within your budget, you can plan and have some idea of where you are going before you get there.

One of the greatest worries for first-time travelers is finding a place to sleep. There are some preparations you should make before you go, but don't get carried away. The trouble with most tourists, and the reason they rarely enjoy their trips, is they are too well-planned. The key is resilience and the ability to adapt and be comfortable in any circumstance.

Many people think low-budget travel requires a lot of "roughing it." On the contrary, there are low-budget hotels, youth hostels, and camping. For the young and the young at heart, there are the ad hoc sleeping arrangements: Finding a place to lay your head down at the last moment. I have found wonderful places to sleep that appeared just when I needed them. They were not three-star hotels, but they were perfect for the atmosphere. I've slept in abandoned churches in the former Yugoslavia, freight trains in Greece, public swimming pools in France, under bridges in Austria, under the stars in just about every region of the world, and even atop the Cheops pyramid in Egypt and on the top of Temple IV at Tikal in Guatemala. No matter where you will find yourself at the end of the day, there will always be a place where you can rest for the night. All you need to do is be prepared with a sleeping bag and an emergency store of food and you are ready to sleep anywhere.

That said, I admit the above paragraph came from the first two editions of this book. Now that I am older, I usually like to plan ahead, a little. To ensure you have a bed at the end of the day, and one that is within your budget, you can plan and have some idea of where you are going before you get there. There are a plethora of apps and websites available to plan your accommodation and the increasingly ubiquitous Airbnb. I rarely book a hotel without reading the advice on TripAdvisor.com.

Planning ahead

There are numerous sources to draw upon when planning where to stay: the guidebook, the traveler's grapevine, and friends and their friends, and of course the internet through websites and apps such as Expedia.com, booking.com and Rocketmiles. I usually check through each of these three to compare prices. Lately I have found that booking.com has the best rates and having talked to hotel staff about this I believe this is because the company charges them the least commission. Rocketmiles is great because you can receive at least 1,000 miles (on an airline of your choice) for each night of your stay.

There also are several good traveler's guidebooks on the market with lists of accommodations for every budget. One of the best is the *Lonely Planet* series, published in Australia by Tony Wheeler and written by a battalion of writers from around the world. Another good one that serves as the de facto bible for travelers in Europe is the *Let's Go* series. They also have books on most other parts of the world. Moon Publications in Chico, California is also good. If you can read French, *Le Guide du Routard* books are excellent sources of travel information as well. Ulysses Press in Berkeley has a good line of books, including a series of publications for women (Such as the Virago Woman's Travel Guides).

When staying in hotels recommended by books like these, you will find other Western travelers staying in the same place. This can be good or bad, depending on how you look at it. It may be nice to speak to someone in your own language and to someone with a similar culture; to exchange insights of the country you are visiting and to get information on the places you plan to visit. However, if you are trying to get into the culture without distractions, you'd be better off avoiding such places.

Ask other travelers about places they've been, and get their impressions of good places to eat, stay and visit. Keep a notebook with you and use it to keep an updated guidebook. If you find any good places on your own, jot them down so you can share them with other travelers. When you get a good collection of places to eat, sleep and visit, send them to Lonely Planet and Let's Go. If they can use them, you will get a free copy of the guide of your choice.

Airbnb offers a great opportunity to sink into the local culture, especially if you choose the room in a home option. Even if you rent an entire place to yourself, your interaction with the owner, and exposure to neighbors, will present a more realistic travel experience than if you stay at the local Sheraton surrounded by foreigners. For about a year in Geneva, I rented out a few rooms in my house on Airbnb, both to earn some extra cash and to meet travelers from all over the world.

The arrival

Often the first impression of a country is intimidating, especially if you arrive by air into a country in the developing world. There you are, backpack in hand, standing on a sidewalk in front of a busy airport. Taxis are lined up by the hundreds, and you're accosted by everyone and his nephew trying to sell you something. All you need is to find a place to crash and rest off the jet lag.

What do you do? If you know of a place, such as those in the guidebooks, you can simply ask directions and go (or use the GPS on your smartphone). In most cities, there is a city bus that goes to the airport, but unless you are already a seasoned traveler, it is best to take a cab or Uber. The brilliance of Uber of course is that you don't need cash and the driver automatically knows your destination. Plus, you can follow the trip on the GPS, so you know the driver is not taking you on a nice long circuitous route. If you are taking a local taxi, be sure to negotiate the price before you depart.

Be sure to negotiate the price as much as possible and look at your room before paying for it.

When you have absolutely no idea where you are going to stay, and you arrive in a big city, like say, Cairo, then what do you do? Again, don't panic. Ask a few locals where to find a hotel and be sure to tell them what price range you are looking for (otherwise they will probably point you toward the Hilton).

Get three or four recommendations and then check them all out. Be sure to negotiate the price as much as possible and look at your room before paying for it. If it is late at night, you may want to grit your teeth and sleep in a place that is less than perfect for your tastes, and then move on when the sun rises.

I arrived in Rio de Janeiro in June 1992 with 30,000 other people to attend and report on the United Nations Conference on Environment and Development for two weeks. The few hotels that were not already booked had doubled their rates. I did not have a reservation and landed at the airport on a flight from Manaus wondering where I was going to stay. I asked around at the airport, talking to the locals who worked there, explaining that I was a reporter from Los Angeles without much money, and needed a place to call home for a month. Within half an hour, I found an apartment with a kitchen, television, bathroom, and living room for twenty dollars a day—less than half what the cheapest hotels were charging.

Youth hostels

Most youth hostels are in the developed world and range from the luxurious to the most Spartan. In Germany, there are hostels that have been open for eighty years. Many hostels outside of Europe are in the least likely of places. In Syria, there is one in a rebuilt twelfth-century Crusader castle. Israel has thirty hostels, and Japan 600. In Australia, there are more than 100 and most of them are good. Most large cities in South America have good youth hostels.

Perched on a cliff on the central California coast, the 115-foot high Pigeon Point Lighthouse has guided mariners since 1872. A youth hostel there offers comfortable, affordable lodgings in four houses set just beside the lighthouse. Guests enjoy cozy indoor lounges, fully equipped kitchens, cove beaches, tidepools, and an oceanfront boardwalk. It is much better and much more reasonably priced than many of the hotels along the coast.

Hosteling International (HI), formerly known as the International Youth Hostel Federation, is a charity that manages a federation of 4,000 not-for-profit youth hostel associations in more than eighty countries. HI's stated belief is that exploration and travel lead to a better understanding of other cultures, which in turn creates a peaceful, smarter, and more tolerant world. Book your hostel stay on hihostels.com.

The kibbutz

A visit to Israel would not be complete without the kibbutz experience. A kibbutz is a commune where everyone works for the good of the community. They accept volunteers who are between the ages of eighteen and forty. As a volunteer on a kibbutz, you may get a job working on the farm, in the laundry, the kitchen, or any of a number of places.

There is usually not any pay for this work, but you get free room and board. You work perhaps four to six hours a day. There is a cafeteria with large buffet-style meals, a coffee house, a theater, and sometimes a bar and disco. Nothing is charged. They even give you stamps and stationery, so you can keep in touch with family.

In 2010, there were 270 kibbutzim in Israel—their factories and farms account for nine percent of Israel's industrial output, worth US$8 billion, and forty percent of its agricultural output, worth over $1.7 billion. If you are interested in pursuing this experience in Israel, call the Jewish Federation in your area and ask for Kibbutz Aliyah Desk, or visit www.kibbutzprogramcenter.net/

Camping

Sleeping in the great outdoors is wonderful no matter where you are, but there are places where you should avoid camping. Europe is one of the best places to camp and usually the most secure. Many travelers tour Europe on bicycle and camp every night.

In most parts of poorer countries, it is unwise to camp anywhere near towns or habitation. I've met many travelers who have awakened to find their valuables stolen—sometimes with the back of their sleeping bags slit open and money belts missing. Unless you are in a designated camp site, be very careful.

When camping, make sure that you are prepared. In most tropical areas you will need a mosquito net, especially if you do not have a tent. In the tropical regions of South America, it is a good idea to travel with a hammock. If you plan to cook, bring a portable stove.

In most countries it is illegal to sleep outside of designated camping areas. The only trouble with these is that they are also full of other campers. If solitude and a good night's rest are what you're after, you may need to search out other spots.

If you leave early enough in the morning, you can camp just about anywhere, provided you know the law and are aware of the risks. If it looks as if it may be someone's front yard, ask for permission and perhaps offer to do a bit of work in exchange. When you depart, leave the grounds as you found them.

If you are going to do any back-country exploring, camping may be your only option. Remember the Boy Scout motto and be prepared, even if you are just heading up the Inca Trail for four days to Machu Picchu. While in the outback, be sensitive to the environment. Take only pictures and leave only footprints.

Make sure you have all the necessary equipment if you are heading into the mountains. Improper preparation can lead to serious complications, injury, and death in extreme circumstances. Never head "into the wild" alone, unless you are properly trained.

Never head "into the wild" alone, unless you are properly trained.

Invitations

By far the most memorable accommodations will be with people you meet in the countries you visit. In the poorer countries of the world people are, in general, more hospitable than in developed countries. Families with nearly nothing in the way of material possessions will invite you into their homes and offer you food. More often than not they will invite you to stay. You will meet your hosts in buses or in markets and through casual acquaintances. Some of them will become the best friends you will ever meet.

When you accept an invitation into someone's home, do so with the utmost of respect. Know that what you are accepting is an honor and should be treated as such. Do your best to observe all local customs and etiquette, and use the experience to become more familiar with the culture (i.e. taking your shoes off, eating only with your right hand, not pointing the souls of your feet at anyone, etc.).

If you are staying more than one night, it is a good idea to contribute something to the household. This has to be done subtly, because the family will probably vehemently turn down any offers. Buy vegetables and goods from the market and give them to the mother (once you've paid for it, it's too late to take it back).

A good way to return the favor in poorer countries is to take pictures of the family and send them copies. Be sure to get a couple with yourself in them, so they will have a memento of your visit.

Often these people will tell you about relatives and friends in other parts of the country. I've met people in Bangladesh and had a place to stay in Bangkok. Don't be shy about looking these people up; they will be more than glad to take you in, and will want to hear of their friends and family you've just visited. Quite often you will meet other travelers on the road, with whom you will exchange addresses and probably stay with when you are in their area. Don't be bashful about calling them: They will look you up when they get to your town.

Renting

If you are going to stay in one place for a while, consider renting a house for an extended period. This will not only be much cheaper than staying in a hotel, it will make you more "local" and will enable you to develop friendships that will give you a deeper insight into the country. For economic reasons, it is most practical to rent a house if you have a family or are with friends you can share the rent with.

If you are going to stay in one place for a while, consider renting a house for an extended period.

Check in with a local real estate office and ask them what they have available. Also check Airbnb for longer term rentals—most places offer big discounts for long-term stays. You can try asking friends you may know in the area. Be careful of any direct contacts that do not go through established intermediaries like Airbnb. There are many charlatans online renting nonexistent rooms and apartments; they take your money through Western Union or other ways and then disappear. Many of these criminals troll places like Craigslist looking for naïve travelers.

When renting an apartment or house for a longer period, avoid renting a place downtown, like in central Paris or Madrid. You can find much nicer places for half the price in the suburbs or in a nearby town.

Russian roulette

American traveler Don Ewing wanted to go to Russia but had no idea of where to stay. He ran an ad in an English-language publication in Russia that read: "Friendly 40-year-old American man requires simple accommodations in your home. Will pay $10 a day."

Ewin received more than seventy letters in two weeks. He spent two weeks each in three of them and had the experiential travel experience he would have missed had he gone through the organized tourist bureau.

Most countries do have English-language publications. Call or write the tourist bureaus of the countries you plan to visit and ask for the addresses of English-language magazines or newspapers. Plan a few months ahead and be prepared for response! If you do arrange something, bring some small gifts from home for your hosts.

Home exchanges

Home exchanging is an inexpensive and convenient way to live close to the people in another country. Home exchange simply means that you and your family agree with a family from a different area to live in each other's homes during your holiday. Swap your home and travel (just about) everywhere in the world. There are several agencies that arrange this service, and publish directories that inform members where they can travel and stay. This is of course only possible if you have a home that you can offer in exchange.

Intervac (us.intervac-homeexchange.com) claims to be the original largest home exchange network in the world with 30,000 members and agents in forty-five countries. It was started in Europe in the early 1950s by a group of teachers with plenty of vacation time looking for economic means to travel internationally. Another service is Home Exchange (www.homeexchange.com), which claims to be the number one home exchange service with 65,000 homes in 150 countries. I traded my apartment in Manhattan once for a one-month stay in a flat in Paris through Home Exchange. They had kids about the same age as mine, and thus both places were kid-proofed with toys.

Servas

Servas is an Esperanto word that means something like "open doors," And Servas.org is an international nonprofit organization, "dedicated to world peace through cultural exchange." What exactly does that mean for its members? Well, long before there was Airbnb or Couchsurfing, travelers could explore the world and stay for free with voluntary Servas hosts around the world for up to two nights.

The Servas website states:

> The purpose of the network is to help build world peace, good-will, and understanding by providing opportunities for personal contacts among people of different cultures, backgrounds and nationalities. Servas promotes trust, tolerance, open-minded-ness, and respect, so that people can live in peaceful coexistence. Our members value understanding of different cultures, gender equality, and diversity in ethnicity, ideology, sexuality, and nationality. In times of globalization and increased movement of people around the planet, there is a growing need to promote understanding across borders and cultures. Hospitality and cultural interaction are the essential tools for achieving conditions for people to live in peace and unity.

Couchsurfing

Couchsurfing is a hospitality and social networking service accessible via a website and mobile app. It was conceived by computer programmer and New Hampshire native Casey Fenton in 1999, when he was 21 years old during a trip to Iceland. He arrived in Reykjavik with no place to stay. Hacking into the university database, he emailed 1,500 students with a request for a place to stay, and received 100 offers. As soon as he returned to the States, he registered the domain www.couchsurfing.com

Members can use the service to arrange homestays, offer lodging and hospitality, and join events such as "Couch Crashes." The platform is a gift economy; hosts are not allowed to charge for lodging. However, unless members have hosted in the previous three months or less they pay an annual fee of €19-55, referred to as "verification," they are only able to send ten new messages per week. Members can either directly request lodging from other members or post their travel plans publicly and receive offers from other members.

Staying on university campuses

In-between semesters most universities and colleges around the world are quiet with hundreds of empty beds. These can be very comfortable places to stay and are often within walking distance of numerous cultural attractions. You don't have to be a student or even around the typical college age group to stay at a college residence and children are sometimes welcome too. Colleges that rent out dorm rooms clear out and clean the residences, so they are ready for guests. The rooms vary as much as the people welcome to stay there: A mix of rooms for one, two, or an entire family are available, and some even come with breakfast provided or an en suite bathroom. You might need to pack a little extra, however. Some might require you to bring your own kitchen utensils, cookware, bedding, and towels.

One way to find out if a university rents out rooms is to visit their website and/or call their director of housing (contact usually available on the website). If you know you want to spend a week in Tucson, for instance, visit the University of Arizona website and see if they have summer housing options.

Another way to find out which universities have summer housing rentals is to visit websites that specialize in these types of bookings. One excellent site is UniversityRooms.com. It offers lodging at universities worldwide, complete with photos, detailed descriptions, and a narrative on what to expect when you arrive.

Hotel Safety Tips

After a long journey you will probably be tired, sore, dirty, and ready to crash. Arriving at your hotel you may have the tendency to let your guard down – don't. The following are a few key hotel safety tips to keep in mind.

Upon arrival

» Stay with your luggage – if you walk into the lobby ahead of your luggage, it might get stolen. Always keep your luggage within eyesight – or even better, touching your leg or strung over your shoulder.

» Ask for a floor between the third and sixth floors. Floors too close to the ground are easier to break into, and those above the sixth floor may not be reachable by fire engine ladders in case of emergency.

At the reception

» Be careful that the receptionist does not say your room out too loud. If you think someone standing in the lobby overheard, ask to be given another room. You never know who is listening and your room number is a matter of personal security.

» Be careful not to lay down your credit card on the counter –a potential thief could capture the numbers with a good camera. When it's handed back to you, double check it's your credit card.

» Ask for two business cards with the hotel name and address. Place one by the phone in your room. If there is an emergency, and you call for help, you'll have the name and address of your location. Keep the other card with you. If you must take a cab or get lost, you can show the driver your location – this is especially useful if the card has the local language on the back (for example, Chinese or Arabic).

In the room
» If a valet has accompanied you to your room, block the door open with a chair or suitcase while you check the room. Look in the closet, in the shower, and behind the curtains before you shut the door or release the valet (in case anyone is hiding there).
» Check the lock to be sure it works. If the door has a deadbolt keep it locked whenever you are in the room. Otherwise, a chair propped up against the doorknob will suffice, or a door wedge. You may want to travel with a door wedge for extra security.
» Place your flashlight or headlamp next to the bed. If there's an alarm or the electricity goes out, you'll have the light you need to find your way around an unfamiliar building.

When you are out of the room
» Always lock up expensive items you won't be carrying with you, such as your laptop or other electronics, in the room safe. Modern hotels with a safe that lets you select your own combination are safer than those with keys. I recommend always carrying your passport with you, in case there is an emergency while you are out in the streets and need to go to your embassy. A friend of mine left his passport in the hotel safe in Port-au-Prince on January 12, 2010. The building collapsed in the earthquake and he had to wait two weeks before it could be recovered.
» If the safe in your room doesn't appear safe, ask the receptionist to lock your valuables in the hotel safe, but ask for a written receipt for the items and ask about the coverage for loss. Most

hotels do not accept liability for items left in the room safes, but they will for those locked in the hotel safe.

» If you lose your key or room entry card, don't take any chances— report it to the hotel immediately and ask to be moved to another room. You can't assume you 'lost' it – it may have been stolen from you by someone whom you do not want showing up at your room in the middle of the night.

Checking out

» If you have things locked in the safe, don't forget to get them when you leave.

» Even if you are confident you collected everything and are leaving nothing behind, double check. Look at every electricity outlet to see if there is a charger, check under the bed and in the closet, and lastly, make sure you did not forget anything in the bathroom. If you are traveling as a couple, or family, get into the habit of everyone checking. If you have kids, give them a small reward if they find anything. If I could count how many times I have left things in hotel rooms, I am sure the number would total up to be more than the pages of this book.

12:

Paying for Things

"A fool and his money are soon parted."
— *English Proverb*

While traveling, you will have to buy things, be it food, souvenirs, or necessities for the road like toothpaste and soap.

While traveling, you will have to buy things, be it food, souvenirs, or necessities for the road like toothpaste and soap. This can be the wallet's point of least resistance and a conduit through which a traveler's hard-earned cash takes flight. Learning how to be frugal and how to negotiate are important travel survival skills.

The entire process of the financial transaction is a cultural trait that differs from country to country. In many places, it is customary to negotiate before paying. Marketplace negotiation is expected protocol, and there is an entire ritual involved.

Unlike Western countries where the shopping process has been sanitized, organized, and computerized, many countries do not put little stickers on the items they sell or identify them with a bar code. This leaves the price to fluctuate on the open market of supply, demand, and the negotiation skills of both the customer and the merchant.

The negotiating process is undertaken with pride and firmness, but with fun and laughter and lightheartedness. If you cannot take the process lightly and have fun with it, you will get nowhere and you will get there quickly.

You start by asking how much something costs, or more commonly: "How much is this worth?" The response will be nowhere near what you should pay. When the merchant in the Gambia responds with "Eighty-five dalases," you put on a look of disbelief, exclaiming: "Eighty-five dalases! Surely, you can let it go for less than that!" (Or something of the like.)

"Well, perhaps I could sell it for eighty, but then I wouldn't be making anything on it, at least no more than a batoot or two." (Don't believe him).

Common cents to getting cash

The days of traveler's checks are long gone. Nowadays you can use a credit card pretty much everywhere. For cash, I always recommend ATMs. Whether you need euros, Swiss francs, shekels, shillings, pesos, or pounds, making a withdrawal from an ATM is generally the

The ATM rate is often significantly better than what you can get from exchanging money at a local exchange counter.

easiest and cheapest way to get cash abroad. The biggest advantage of getting local cash with your ATM card is that all withdrawals, regardless of size, are exchanged based on the wholesale exchange rate, which is usually reserved only for very large interbank exchanges. The ATM rate is often significantly better than what you can get from exchanging money at a local exchange counter, which in addition to the poor rate will often add on transaction fees, which can easily eat up another two percent of your money.

Always pay in the local currency, unless you are absolutely in a bind. Never assume that American dollars will be accepted, and even if they are—paying in dollars sets you apart as an uncaring foreigner who presupposes the local currency is not worth your time. Also, the rates of exchange at impromptu exchanges will be several percentage points higher than at a bank or through an ATM.

When in Rome, do as the Romans: Pay in euro.

Tipping

To tip or not to tip, that is the question – and if the answer is yes, then how much? This has always been one of the great traveler conundrums, as it changes from country to country.

In the United States, servers (waiters and waitresses) depend on tips to survive, and so failing to leave a tip could be considered rude or even cruel. According to the United States Department of Labor website, restaurants in the USA are legally allowed to pay their servers $2.13 an hour – far below the minimum wage and even further below that required to live above the poverty threshold. Thus, the expected tip is between 15 and 20 percent of the pre-tax bill. Some people just look at the amount of tax added and double it.

In Canada, servers earn substantially more for an hourly wage than their counterparts south of the border, but they still expect to receive at least 15 percent of the pre-tax bill amount as a tip. The same is true for Mexico, where people working in the service industries earn very modest salaries and rely on tips to earn a living wage. Generally, one should leave a tip (*una propina*) of between 10 and 15 percent.

In countries outside of North America, however, the tipping culture operates in a different way, with different amounts and policies considered appropriate, depending on the country or region. In Costa Rica, for example, a 10 percent service charge is usually included in the bill, but adding a tip is welcome and appreciated (but not expected).

Most restaurants in Britain will add a service charge to your bill. If there's no service charge (which would be clearly marked on your check), a 10-15 percent tip is considered appropriate.

Across the channel in France, service is almost always "*compris*" (included) but even if it is not, the general rule is to round up the bill, or leave a few euros as a "pourboire" (quite literally, for a drink). In Italy, the common practice was for customers to pay a cover charge before entering a bar or restaurant. This custom known as "pane e coperto," is being phased out and replaced with the ubiquitous service charge, added to your check. If you want to tip more, just round up the bill. This practice of rounding up the bill is pretty much the same across Europe. That said, servers in touristy areas usually get excited when they have American guests because all too often we tip there as at home.

In Switzerland, the servers probably earn more than you and I put together and so they do not generally expect a tip. If you receive amazing service, feel free to round up the bill. If you don't leave anything, it is highly unlikely that your server will chase you down the street to seek an explanation, as might happen in the United States if you stiff your waiter. That said, I find the service in Switzerland inferior to elsewhere because they do not rely on their tips. In the US, in contrast, the servers are constantly checking with you to make sure you are happy with the service.

In Israel, restaurants also itemize the service in the bill – 15 percent. However, if you are pleased with the service, locals always leave a one-shekel tip for each member of the party. In Egypt, higher-end restaurants will usually include a small service change in the final bill, but it's customary to leave an additional 5-10 percent tip in addition.

In the larger cities and more tourist-dense areas of India, tipping is becoming more expected, and many businesses have adopted the practice of adding service charges to the bill. If no such charge has been included, tipping isn't required, but is often deemed courteous. It's also a good idea if you plan to return to the same restaurant.

In China, even in Taiping, tipping isn't typically expected – although in trendy tourist areas the locals are starting to expect it. In Japan, service workers do not expect tips either. In fact, leaving or giving cash as a tip can be considered rude. If you do want to provide a tip be sure to conceal your yen in an envelope before handing it to the server. Elsewhere in Asia, tipping isn't necessary, but service workers will generally be happy to accept a small gratuity. Rounding up the bill will always be appreciated.

Tipping in hotels

While restaurant tipping may change from country to country, I find that it is always good to leave a tip in a hotel – in the range from $2 to $5 per day, depending on the mess you make, how many of you are in the room, etc. Some people wait until the last day to leave a tip, but I find that leaving a little bit every day that you are in the same hotel can greatly improve the quality of service you receive – extra shampoos in the bathroom, etc. Also, in my opinion leaving something for housekeeping is just the right thing to do because they can be considered the lowest in the hotel hierarchy and are quite often the hardest workers.

Also, if a hotel employee brings a towel, an iron, or another useful item to your room they should be given a small tip. This will ensure that the next time you ask for something, he or she will provide the same quality service. If someone carried your bags to your room, I recommend giving a dollar equivalent for each bag.

The language edge

This is where learning the language becomes advantageous. Once you've grasped the language well enough, eavesdrop on local people discussing a sale, and discreetly watch how much they pay. When you know what a local person pays, you are better able to negotiate your price.

I was in Luxor, Egypt, and wanted to buy a rice paper painting at a local curio shop to send to my mother. I sauntered in, the wind chimes hanging behind the door sending a loud jingle through the shop. The shopkeeper was tending an Egyptian woman who was looking at an assortment of paintings on a shelf.

"Very good afternoon sir, I'll be with you in a few moments," he said in a Berlitz-polished British accent.

I walked over to the paintings, and tried to make out as best I could the conversation that was going on in Arabic between the woman and the man.

"Ten pounds!" she exclaimed in her guttural Arabic voice that always seems like it comes from the back of the rib cage.

"All right, eight — but no less. I can't possibly let it go for any less than that."

"I'll take two for 12. Wrap them up."

"But that is only six a piece. I said I can't go any less than eight."

"Fine," she countered. "Then I'll talk to the man across the street. I'm sure he can be more accommodating."

As she closed her handbag and started walking toward the door, he shouted after her: "In the name of Allah, all right. Give me fourteen and you can have them both."

"Twelve and a half. "

"Thirteen."

"Good."

He wrapped up the two paintings and handed them respectfully to the woman. "Go with Allah. "

He then turned to me, asking in English: "What can I sell you today kind sir?"

Picking up a single painting that looked very much like the one the woman had just purchased, I asked him in English how much it sold for.

"Twenty-five each, sir, and that is our extremely-low discounted price."

The transaction

If you don't understand the local lingo well enough to eavesdrop, you can either watch the money change hands, trying to see how much is being paid (but this can be difficult), or find a local friend and ask him how much you should pay for it.

Once you know what the price is, never go in and offer that price right away or the shop keeper may lose face and forfeit the sale. Ask him or her first how much it costs, and then negotiate your price. Your counter offer should be lower than what you expect to pay, so that you can come up gradually as your negotiating partner slowly drops his price down. The end price should be a win-win situation for both of you, if one of you leaves the interaction feeling bad, it was not good business.

As a foreigner, you will be at an immediate disadvantage when it comes to buying things. You can expect that when a local asks for a price, he or she will be told something that is roughly twenty-five percent higher than what should be paid. But as a foreigner, the spread may be closer to fifty to 100 percent.

Don't take this personally; it is easy to get bent out of shape at this apparent discriminating opportunism, but you will need to get used to it. Many people around the world who don't know who you are will automatically think that you have got a tree back home that

As a foreigner, you will be at an immediate disadvantage when it comes to buying things.

grows money, that your streets are paved with gold, and that you can afford to pay more because, after all, you are a foreigner.

But no, you shouldn't pay more. Some tourists justify paying higher prices as a contribution to the local economy. This has a detrimental effect by causing artificial inflation.

When a group of tourists arrives in a small village that happens to be situated outside some newly discovered ruins, they often buy things without negotiating and pay the inflated prices. When the shopkeepers discover they can get 3,000 pesos for an orange instead of the usual 1,000, they will begin holding out selling them until they can get 3,000. When a local family man comes along with a pocket full of 2,000 pesos to buy oranges for his two kids, he can't find anyone to sell them to him because they are all holding out for bigger profits.

Comparison shopping

When you have absolutely no idea how much something should cost, and there is no one in the shop buying what you want, a good scheme that always works is comparison shopping.

For example, if you want to buy a bottle of shampoo at a small shop in Guatemala and have no idea how much it should cost, you look for something that you do know the price of. Just the day before you may have purchased a bar of soap from the store down the road and the price was four quetzales.

You ask how much the soap costs, and when the shop keeper responds with "eight quetzales," you know that he is doubling his prices for the unsuspecting Gringo. You can then ask how much the shampoo is. If he says "twenty quetzales," you can bet the real price is somewhere around ten.

If the merchant will not let an item go for the price you know you should pay, simply walk out with a shrug. If he wants to make the sale bad enough he'll come running after you. If he doesn't, he either does not want to make the sale or you underbid.

Taking taxis

Taxis the world over are notorious for ripping off foreigners. The most common way is to put on the meter and take you for a zig-zag route all over town on the way to your destination. What should have cost you 20,000 won for a ride across town in Seoul, ended up being 50,000. What do you do in this situation? You pay. You've been taken for a ride (literally) and you would be in the wrong if you did not pay. After all, he didn't know you were not interested in the scenic route.

The best way to avoid this is to find out from a friendly local how much a trip should cost before you set off to your destination. If you can get the cab to take you there for that amount, you've got it made. Otherwise, it's time for plan B: Sit yourself in the front seat (if you are alone), and take out your map or smartphone GPS. Locate where you are and where you want to go. Let the driver know that you are going to follow the route on the map along the way, but do it in a manner that won't offend him with an assumption that he is going to rip you off. Just tell him that you are interested in the city, and would like him to point things out to you on the map along the way.

If you are unfamiliar with the city, it is a good idea to do this anyway. In some cities, the driver may simply take you to a bad part of town away from police and rip you off at gun point.

If you don't have a map or smartphone, don't know how much it should cost, and have no idea where you are, try to make it look as though you are familiar with the city and its ways. Be relaxed and confident and talk to the driver as if he were a friend. He will probably think twice about ripping you off if he thinks you are already familiar with his city.

In Rio de Janeiro the inflation is so bad the taxis have meters with several decimal points and a special government-issued rate conversion chart to translate the numbers on the meter. The numbers on the chart are less than on the meter, so you need to know about it if you want to avoid paying too much. Often the driver will tell you the meter does not work, or that the policy was changed "just this morning." Don't believe him/her. Get out of the cab and find another. If he wants your business bad enough, he'll suddenly remember the truth.

Another thing to keep in mind when taking taxis is the poltergeist meter. While in a cab in Rio I kept my eye on the meter to make sure it didn't go past the amount of cash I had in my pocket. I looked out my side window for a second and when I looked back at the meter it had suddenly jumped several thousand cruzeiros (about two dollars). When I asked him what happened, the driver merely shrugged and said it must be broken. When we arrived at my destination, we both agreed that the final price was about ten thousand cruzeiros too high. I have heard stories of taxi drivers hooking the meters up to their horns, or even the radio. If your driver is honking his horn a lot, or keeps switching radio stations, keep an eye on the meter.

Although controversial among some people, I love Uber for international travel. The account is connected to a credit or debit card so there is no cash transaction, and you always get a trip estimate before setting off. The cars are usually clean and new. I have walked out of meetings in Shanghai or Barcelona, pulled out my iPhone, clicked on Uber, and typed in my destination. A driver pulls up a few minutes later and he already knows my name.

13:

Keeping in Touch
While on the Move

"...from whatever place I write
you will expect that a part of my "travels"
will consist of excursions in my own mind."

— *S.T. Coleridge*

Although email is increasingly ubiquitous and easier than schlepping to the post office, the folks back home may really appreciate getting an old-school post card.

While waiting in a short line to check my mail at the American Express office in Kathmandu, I observed an American at the counter get into a cross-cultural conflict with the clerk. The American had announced that his last name was Zachary, and that it started with a "zee." The Nepali proceeded to look through the "c's," and told Mr. Zachary that he had no mail. Feeling just a bit perturbed, as happens in such cases when you are unable to step back and see who's really at fault, the American increased the volume of his voice and demanded that the Nepali look under "zee" and not "cee."

"But I have looked under 'c', exactly as you just told me," replied the Nepali, starting to get perplexed and lose his patience.

"No, I said 'zee,' as in 'zeebra,'" he said, expecting the Nepali to be familiar with the American pronunciation of both words.

"Oh, I see," the clerk replied. "You mean 'zed,' as in 'zebra.' Let me check that letter for you.'"

The traveler left with not only his mail, but two very important realizations: First, that Americans are the only English speakers in the world who pronounce "z" as "zee" instead of "zed." And secondly, that you cannot assume anything when it comes to thinking others may see things the way you do.

Mail-dominated societies

When I was first exploring the world in the 1980s, staying in touch or getting in touch with loved ones and friends back home was a real challenge—it could take days just to make a phone call. Now, in the twenty-first century era of smartphones, WhatsApp, and Instagram, the challenge is more about disconnecting, than connecting.

I would have mail sent to the Canadian embassies and high commissions in a country I figured I would visit in three months. I remember arriving at the high commission in Lusaka, Zambia about two months late and receiving more than 100 letters from friends and family around the world. Needless to say, everyone at the embassy was quite impressed when I finally showed up. Everyone knew my name.

I have edited out from previous editions most of the laborious details of how to get mail while traveling (in the 1980s). These days it is probably easiest to just have your mail sent to a hotel, and to make a booking for a night at that hotel. You can also have it sent to you with the words "General Delivery" at the local post office.

Although email is increasingly ubiquitous and easier than schlepping to the post office, the folks back home may really appreciate getting an old-school post card. During my long five-year trip around the world, I tried to send my grandmother a post card every month. She collected them all on her wall and showed them off to her friends. I know this meant a lot to her. Plus, when I returned and moved in with her to finish my bachelor's degree, she had them all bound up in a book and gave them back to me. I still look at them occasionally as a travelogue and as a special memento of the special relationship I had with her.

Recently while in Paris, I found a stand selling unique postcards of Parisian scenes with cats. Knowing that my mother is the quintessential cat lady, I bought a dozen of them, and posted one each day to her in Canada. A small effort and a low cost to send an invaluable message to my mom that I love her and think of her every day (had I paid with Mastercard it would have made a perfect "Priceless" advertisement).

Sending stuff home

While you may not be interested in receiving a letter or package, you may want to occasionally send packages of special souvenirs back home, so you will not have to pack them around with you. Or you may want to send presents on birthdays and special holidays to remind people you still exist. The memorabilia you send back will mean a lot to you in the future like gifts families presented you with, small carvings, etc.

If you don't care when your package arrives, send it by land. Sending boxes to the United States or Canada used to take up to six months from more remote countries and a month or two from Europe.

Get a solid box and put everything you are sending into a plastic bag to insulate it from moisture. Write the address on the inside as well as the outside, and make sure it is well taped up. Be prepared to declare the contents at the post office. In India, it used to be the case that the entire package had to be sewn up in white cotton and then sealed with wax seals along the seams. To provide this service, there was a battalion of tailors on the sidewalk in front of every post office. Each had his or her unique seal.

Whenever you send something from a post office, it is a good idea to check that the postal clerk cancels the stamp in front of you. To ask this may seem insulting, and perhaps it is to some postal employees, but I have heard of cases where the clerk simply peeled off the stamp to sell it again, slipping the ill-gotten profit into his pocket.

While you are buying gifts for your friends and family back home, you may want to think of investing some money in souvenirs for resale value. Carvings, jewelry, and batiks all can triple, quadruple, or better their investments anywhere people have a love affair with the exotic (which is most everywhere). I know of travelers who lived quite well in Japan on profits from small carvings and paintings they had bought in India and shipped to a prearranged Tokyo address.

If you do this, be aware of customs and import restrictions.

Receiving money while abroad

While you may not be too interested in receiving a letter or package while traveling, if you run out of money you may need to have an

If you run out of money you may need to have an emergency transfusion from a rich friend back home.

emergency transfusion from a rich friend back home. My preference is to carry an ATM debit card linked to a bank where someone can simply deposit some cash or wire transfer some funds. Another option is the tried and true Western Union, although their exorbitant rates may deter you.

Letting your fingers do the walking

Phone calls used to be a real headache, depending on the country you are calling to and from. In some countries you had to go to a telephone service and tell a person over the counter where you want to call. You were then told to take a seat and when it was finally put through your name was called. This could be either a half hour or a half day. In one case while waiting to hear about my grandfather's health while I was in Khartoum, it took three days.

In Europe and in emerging market countries like Turkey and Thailand, you can call home from payphones with little or no hassle. However, in the age of smartphones and other mobile devices, the payphone is quickly going the way of the eight-track tape and computer floppy disks. Many payphones around the world now require small "telecards" when making a call. These small cards are about the size of an American driver's license and are available at most post offices. You buy a card that is worth a certain number of calls. The card is then inserted into a phone, and credits are deducted when you complete your call.

When you make long distance calls, be sure to consult the world time zone chart. You'll want to call when it is most convenient for the person you are calling so he or she will be coherent enough to have a conversation. I've called home a couple of times forgetting it was 4 a.m. there and then wasted five minutes until my mother or sister were awake enough to know it was me.

If you are of the generation that is leapfrogging payphones, I am sure you are already familiar with the numerous VOIP (Voice Over Internet Protocol) applications that are now available—many with videocall streaming capability. My preferred video calling apps are FaceTime on the Apple iOS, or LINE, WhatsApp, and WeChat on either Apple or Android. If you do use these, be careful to monitor your data plan, choose a good roaming option with your home service, buy a prepaid local simcard, or use them only at restaurants or hotels with free Wi-Fi.

Online blogs and vlogs

There's no better way to keep your friends back home up to date with your travels than keeping a blog—or a video blog (a vlog).

With a blog you can write something that all your friends, family and "followers" can read, without having to spend hours sending emails to each one. You can include photos or videos or links to places you've visited or stayed, and you can update it easily and regularly.

Modern technology makes it easy to spew unlimited and unedited insights so that others can follow our journey from country to country around the world. However, to ensure that people will want to read your blog (beyond your grandmother or mother) here are a few things to keep in mind when writing an online travel diary that others will want to follow.

Keep it succinct. We all want to know what you're doing on your travels, but we don't want to know everything. Avoid details like "We got up at 6.30 am and had a shower …". We don't need to know what you eat for each meal. You might write about a museum exhibition that particularly impressed you or describe an unusual local you met on the street. Amanda Kendle of vagabondish.com likes to describe the very best and the very worst of a journey, because "somehow that's what everybody really wants to know."

A photo is worth a thousand words. If you have an eye for photography, be sure to include photos or even videos to your travel blog. A couple of photos are especially useful if you're describing something we might not have seen before. Be selective—we are not interested in scrolling through a hundred photos of your visit to the Louvre, and we definitely do not need to see images of every meal you eat while away.

One thing I have done for the past couple of years is photograph a flower every day, wherever I am in the world, trying to capture the image in a unique way and within the context of its local surroundings. I do this for my mother and tag each photo on Instagram as #dailyFlowers4Mom.

Link it up. Be sure to include some links (for example to the website of the art gallery you visited), if you think the site is worth looking at for people who are interested to find out more.

Update regularly. Once you capture someone's interest with your succinct writing and colorful photos, keep them hooked by writing regularly. Of course, you won't have any internet access when you're mid-Sahara on a week-long journey in an old truck. Or you might be visiting a country where internet access is ridiculously expensive and decide to limit your online time. But do what you can to keep your readers updated. If you don't think you can find time to write your blog, don't start one.

Get started the right away. There are some great websites that provide the blogging infrastructure for you. MatadorTravel is one that offers a cool community of travelers as well so you end up getting a lot of great comments and advice on your blog. Their blog format is clean, and your friends can subscribe to your blog and get alerts when you update it. matadortravel.com/create

Follow other bloggers. To get a better idea of how to write a good blog, read other travel blogs. The June 9 edition of *Wanderlust Travel Magazine* included a list of the most important, useful, and entertaining travel blogs it believes every traveler should be following.

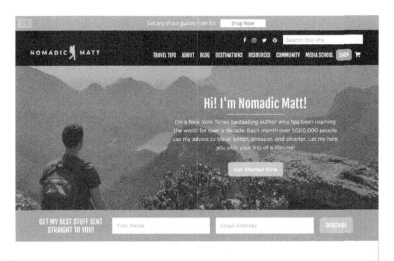

Latest from the Blog

OVERTOURISM: HOW YOU CAN HELP SOLVE THIS WORLDWIDE PROBLEM

THE STUDENTS FROM THE VICTOR SCHOOL RETURN FROM GUATEMALA. HERE'S THE RECAP!

THE SATURDAY CITY: STOCKHOLM

www.nomadicmatt.com

Foremost among these is *Stuck in Customs* (stuckincustoms.com), which showcases Trey Ratcliff's amazing travel photos. Of most interest to aspiring photographers are the step-by-step guides to how he took them. His guide to HDR photography is arguably one of the best on the web. A few others travel bloggers you may appreciate:

» Nomadic Matt is the *New York Times* best-selling author of *How to Travel the World on $50 a Day* and founder of his own blog at www.nomadicmatt.com. He claims that each month more than a million travelers use his advice to travel better, cheaper, and longer.

» Irish travel blogger Benny Lewis sets language challenges for himself and along the way shows how you too can learn another language cheaply and quickly. You can visit his blog at fluentin3months.com.

» Geraldine DeRuiter travels the world and eats, and eats, and eats. She is also the author of the book, *All Over the Place: Adventures in Travel, True Love, and Petty Theft*. But she's not your average travel foodie blogger, as exemplified by posts like "7 Badass Bavarian Foods You Must Try." Visit her blog at everywhereist.com.

» Anil Polat focuses on technology in his travel blog, providing an up-to-the-minute advice on wireless internet on the road, international SIM cards, and exactly which chargers you should be taking with you. Connect with Anil at foxnomad.com.

» Heralded as the premier travel resource for women, Evelyn Hannon's blog at journeywoman.com tackles everything from packing to traveling safely—with lots of good food in between.

Your blog does not have to be as commercially oriented as these but reading them can give you some ideas as you form your own unique voice and expression for your blog.

14:

Food

"Never journey without something
to eat in your pocket. If only to throw at
the dogs when attacked by them."

— *E. S. Bates*

Eating offers one of the finest aspects of traveling. Part of a country's culture is found in the way it feeds itself.

Eating offers one of the finest aspects of traveling. Part of a country's culture is found in the way it feeds itself. The best way to truly partake of the traveler's banquet while on the road is to be adventurous: Bring a big plate and don't be bashful about trying new dishes.

The first thing I do when I arrive in a country is go to the market to see what there is to eat. At a restaurant, I look around at the other tables to see what everyone else is eating, and then order what looks best. This can be extremely rewarding and adventurous.

Trying new foods will often leave your taste buds in euphoric bliss. The possibilities are endless: In some countries, especially in Asia, you can spend your entire vacation eating and not have the same thing twice! I can never understand how people can lose weight while traveling when there is a veritable banquet on every corner.

In the tropics it is very likely that you'll become a fruitarian. A trip to the market will yield a cornucopia of tropical delights. When buying fruit and vegetables, remember that things with peels can be eaten on the spot, but anything else should be taken back to your room and soaked in the sink for at least twenty minutes in a mixture of water and iodine or bleach to disinfect them.

Restaurant, café, or street food?

To avoid the dreaded Delhi Belly, or Montezuma's revenge, exercise precaution when choosing your restaurant, café, or sidewalk stall. Is it clean? Are there many people there? What does it smell like? These are all questions you should ask yourself before you walk in and order.

Look for a place that is busy. If a lot of people eat there it means that the food is probably good, and there is a high turnover. Many people eating in the same place is an indication that the food has a higher chance of being fresh and hot. If nobody is there, the food that ends up on your plate could have been prepared yesterday or last week.

Don't be afraid to look in the kitchen. If it is dirty, you may want to walk up the street a bit farther.

Many travelers prefer eating at sidewalk stalls. This makes good sense for many reasons. You can see the food being prepared and thus know if it is fresh and if the stove is clean. The ambiance is often lively and bustling with energy, combining entertainment with a dining experience. Since the cook's overhead is lower than a restaurant (no rent or salaries), the price is often much cheaper than eating indoors. Often in smaller communities you will see homes with a few tables set up out front. This is popular in the rural areas of Brazil and in Vietnam. To earn an extra income, families will sell meals in front of their houses. The food is usually as good as a home-cooked meal anywhere, and the cost is much lower than a restaurant. If you see a group of people eating in front of a home, approach them discreetly and ask if they are selling meals. If you just sit down and order, there is always the danger of finding yourself in the middle of a family picnic.

In Cuba, families can get a government license to rent rooms to foreigners and another license to sell them food. Once, at the Bay of Pigs, we stayed with a family who had a license to rent, but not to cook. However, with curtains quickly pulled and the lights dimmed down, we had our best Cuban meal of two weeks in the country.

In February 2018 *The Independent* newspaper of Britain published a story of a street-food vendor in Thailand who was awarded the highly coveted Michelin star for her crab omelette. There is now a four-hour wait to taste the street food cooked by this eccentric 72-year-old women, who wears ski goggles to protect her eyes. Just north of Copenhagen, at the Kronborg Castle, home of Shakespeare's Hamlet, street food venders have been organized in a giant warehouse, where they park their trucks and sell to tourists.

Many travelers prefer eating at sidewalk stalls.

As a guest

I do believe you have never really been to a country if you have not had a local meal with a local person (or family), and have talked about local realities while "breaking bread." You can accomplish this by inviting someone to dinner, and asking them to recommend a place, or being invited into someone's home. The latter is of course much easier if you have a contact before arriving, but in some countries you will find yourself invited into many homes. Part of this is from sincere invitations, others due to cultural traditions that dictate that all people in the immediate vicinity be invited before one can eat.

Because you are a foreigner, most invitations will probably be sincere, but know when to differentiate. In East Africa, anytime

Enjoying a meal in a hut at the top of the Ngorongoro volcano in Virunga National Park in the Democratic Republic of Congo.

someone passes someone else eating, the person eating says *karibu kula* (welcome to eat). The customary response is *ahsante* (thank you), and then keep walking.

When you are invited into someone's home, exercise discretion as to whether your refusal to eat what your hosts have offered will offend them. In Mexico I was invited into a woman's home for a bowl of menudo (tripe soup). Señora Vasquez had such a look of hopeful anticipation on her face that I couldn't refuse, even though I have chosen not to eat mammals, and on the rare occasion that I do, I try and avoid entrails. She watched me with her expectant brown eyes as I slowly but steadfastly ate the whole thing, at the whole thing, expressing my heartfelt appreciation afterwards.

It is an honor in many countries to have a guest in one's home and likewise an honor to be invited. This is an opportunity to

fine-tune those powers of perception and pay attention to all the little details that make up a culture.Do you take your shoes off at the door? How do they eat? With their hands? If so, in what way? How do you sit? All these questions can be answered through observation.

Health precautions

There is one very important rule to remember when experiencing local cuisine: Though it is good to try one of everything when on the road, remember your health. Even if you go to a place with high hygienic standards, you need to be careful when it comes to what you put into your body. You are what you eat, and if you eat food that should be in the garbage, that is exactly how you are going to feel if you eat it.

Your health is your most important asset while on the road. Be sure to eat well, and don't cut any corners when your budget is tight. If you find yourself skipping meals to save money, it may be time to go home.

Make sure the food you eat is freshly cooked and hot, or that you have peeled it yourself if it is a fruit or vegetable. You can soak vegetables in a sink with iodine or bleach to kill any bacteria there may be lurking. Seven to ten drops in a sink full of water should suffice.

Watch out for the ice. Many people buy bottled drinks and pour them into glasses full of ice cubes. If you do this in some countries, be prepared to catch up on your reading in the bathroom.

The emergency stash

Always keep an emergency stash of food at the bottom of your pack or suitcase. This is especially important if you are traveling with kids. I always had a few cans of sardines with me for emergency use as well as some instant coffee and a few tea bags. Peanut butter is a great source of protein and can make even stale bread remind you of home. Try mixing it some with honey. Sardines are available anywhere in the world and do wonders to spice up a plate of rice or stack of bread. I like to carry a few small containers with spices like salt and pepper (pre-mixed) and chili flakes.

Hands or utensils?

One of the first things you will notice is that people in different parts of the world have figured out different ways to get the food from plates or bowls into their mouths. No one way is better than the other; they are all just different. The options are tools or hands, and it is part of the travel experience to adapt to whatever the social norm happens to be in the area you are visiting. Be adventurous and dig in with your fingers if that is what you see your hosts doing. You may even discover that some foods actually taste better when you eat them with your hand. To me, both Ethiopian and Indian food taste better when consumed with fingers, than with forks. I have no idea why.

One reason perhaps can be explained by the ancient Vedic texts of India, which state that eating should be a sensory experience filled with emotion and passion. These scriptures describe how every finger is an extension of the five elements: Through the thumb comes space, with the forefinger comes air, the middle finger is fire, the ring finger is water, and the little finger represents earth. Thus, using one's fingers to eat stimulates these five elements and helps in bringing forth digestive juices in the stomach.

Calling upon more allopathic interpretations for fingers and food we find that the nerve endings on our fingertips can stimulate digestion. Feeling your food becomes a way of signaling the stomach that you are about to eat, and you become more conscious of the taste, textures, and aromas.

There are many ways to eat with your hands. Just when you get used to one, you'll travel somewhere else and the custom will change. What doesn't change however is that you never, under any circumstances, touch the food with your left hand. The left hand is considered unclean and is only used for other less sanitary tasks.

Sticks and stones

Many of us in the West have learned how to use chopsticks because Chinese food has become about as familiar to us as Colonel Sanders. If you haven't yet learned how to use them, get yourself a pair and ask someone to show you the basics.

When you get the technique down, practice picking up small stones in your room. The muscles in your hands will be sore at first, but before long, eating with chopsticks will become second nature and you'll be catching flies like Bruce Lee.

The times when you eat, and which meal is the main course for the day changes from country to country. In Europe, it is customary to eat only a continental breakfast in the morning, which consists of bread, coffee, and sometimes a glass of juice. This may be difficult to adjust to for those of us who are used to large breakfasts, but again, trying a new way of life is part of the travel experience. If you are still hungry after a continental breakfast, you can always order two or three more with extra bread.

Cooking on your own

A lot of money can be saved by cooking your own food. Unfortunately, this is not as easy as it may first appear. It can be difficult to find all the ingredients you need and to find a place where you can cook. If you can manage all the variables, cooking on your own can be a fun alternative to eating out all the time. Join a friend or small group and you can turn your evening meal into a party.

It is sometimes possible to cook in youth hostels and some hotels that have kitchens. If this is the case, tremendous savings can be made, especially when traveling in Europe. If you are staying in one place for a while, see if there is a refrigerator you can use, and make sure your food is properly marked so it doesn't disappear.

Try to join some people who are staying in the same place for a while and organize a cooking group. This can help cut down on expenses, and you can have a bigger meal. Organize the entire hostel to participate in a pot-luck. This is a great way to meet other travelers.

For vegetarians

It can be difficult to maintain a strict vegetarian diet in many parts of the world. However, if you are committed, there is always a way. As a vegetarian, you must pay very close attention to the food you eat, and constantly monitor your body to ensure you are getting enough protein, vitamins, and amino acids. If you eat a lot of fruit and vegetables, be very careful to clean and sanitize them thoroughly.

One of the biggest sacrifices vegetarian travelers must make is when they are invited into someone's house. In many parts of the world, vegetables and grains are hard to come by, and consequently this means food must be obtained wherever it is available. If a village is situated on the coast or a river, most likely the people will have adapted to eating fish, probably with rice or bread. The way they catch their fish and how they prepare it are an integral part of their culture.

Most villages tend to have flocks of chickens that run about, rummaging through refuse and foraging off weeds and grass. When a visitor is invited into the home, a chicken is caught and slaughtered in his or her honor. Sometimes the menu may include a larger animal, such as a goat or sheep. If you are a vegetarian, be sure to let it be known well ahead of time before the animal is killed.

When you are called upon to explain your dietary preferences, be prepared for an inquisition in some countries. Be careful not to upset local sentiments by inadvertently coming across as being "holier than thou" because you don't eat meat and they do. This will only create hard feelings and will cause walls to go up between you and your hosts. If you want to encourage a healthier diet and one that is better for the planet, rest assured that you are doing so simply by teaching through example.

The best thing to do if you are a strict vegetarian and want to travel in areas where you do not think you'll be able to get adequate non-meat foods is to bring your own. If you bring your own rice, lentils, etc., you should always be able to find someone who can cook them for you. Carry high-protein substances like miso or Vegemite to mix in with grains or to spread on bread. Most things you can buy in the host country; others you will have to bring (or travel with an Australian; they invariably always have jars of Vegemite).

In some parts of the world it is easier to be vegetarian than an omnivore. For strict vegetarians, India is probably the best place to travel. The most difficult is the Middle East, and most of South

America and Africa where meat is mixed in with just about every-thing. Also, surprisingly, in Southeast Asia, when you ask for a veg-etarian meal, like fried rice for example, you may find that it has shrimps and was fried in lard.

When you eat in a restaurant, tell the waiter or waitress that you are a vegetarian. Explain that you do not eat any meat, and that in-cludes chicken and shrimp. In many places, when you say you don't eat meat, they assume you can eat seafood and poultry. If you do not make it clear to them, your "vegetarian plate" will have pieces of meat in it.

In Europe, you should always be able to find vegetarian restau-rants. Check with the local chamber of commerce or look for a Hin-du temple. Hare Krishnas can be found in most parts of the world and can always be relied upon to know about the best vegetarian restaurants in town. If none of the above are available, just ask a few locals. Even if they are not vegetarians, they should be able to point you in the right direction.

Judy Amber Lloyd, director of the Los Angeles office of the veg-etarian organization Earth Save, always carries a kit of food staples with her when traveling. The kit includes trail mix, a simple sprout-ing packet with a variety of beans to sprout, wheat germ, lethicin, Spike seasoning, Braggs Liquid Aminos, and sunflower seeds. If she can't find a vegetarian restaurant, she looks for a restaurant with a good all-you-can-eat buffet stocked with lots of vegetables, salads, and fresh fruit.

Lloyd, originally from New Zealand, traveled for six years in Europe and always found something in a restaurant she could eat. While traveling in developing countries, she takes a bottle of apple cider vinegar (a substitute for iodine) to wash fresh fruit before eat-ing.

15:

Red Tape

"The border means more than a customs house, a passport officer, a man with a gun. Over there everything is going to be different; life is never going to be quite the same again after your passport has been stamped and you find yourself speechless among the money-changers."

— *Graham Greene*

Crossing the border is always the best time to put on your best clothes and be on your best behavior.

At a small cluster of huts at what looked like the outer reaches of an unnamed fishing village, our small boat reeled toward shore and moored against a muddy embankment in the heart of the Amazon rainforest. We had just traveled for twelve hours down the river from Iquitos, Peru and now needed to cross over into Brazil.

The captain jumped ashore with a rope, motioning for the eighteen Peruvian and Brazilian passengers and me to disembark. We walked down a winding trail to a bamboo fence. Inside was a large marshy yard with an elevated sidewalk separating our steps from a cacophony of croaking frogs. The walkway led to a dilapidated structure that presumably served as the immigration office.

Inside the house was an office with a large desk, and an even larger drunken official seated behind it. The first fellow traveler walked in and presented his passport and other identification. The official scowled, extracted some payment, and then issued the necessary exit visa. One at a time, a Peruvian would walk in, meekly state his request, pay a special fee and leave with his stamp.

While I was waiting, I read a collage of notices that was pasted haphazardly on the wall. One of them announced and described the three enemies of humanity: Tobacco, drugs, and alcohol. These three, it stated, brought on corruption, violence, laziness, and ineptitude.

It was my turn. I looked out the open window and noticed the sun had set. A single oil-fueled lantern illuminated the room, casting dancing shadows across a dusty floor. I walked in, my attention immediately drawn to a sign in Spanish on the wall behind the official that read: "Your rights end where mine begin."

"Great," I thought to myself, as I took a deep breath to remain calm.

My eyes dropped to the desk and focused on a form in uniform sprawled across his paperwork—passed out. I looked over at his rather young, attractive, and scantily-dressed but gratefully sober assistant who motioned for me to keep cool while she took my papers and stamped them. With an apologetic look she handed them back to me and said I could go, wishing me a safe journey.

The ubiquitous bureaucracy

No matter where you travel, you will run into the ubiquitous bureaucrat. Making sure you have all the proper paperwork in order when dealing with officials will prevent many headaches.

In getting your paperwork done, you will have to wrestle with a lot of bureaucracy and dealing effectively with it takes foresight, ingenuity, a bit of audacity, and a whole lot of patience.

Plan ahead anytime you think you might be confronted with officialdom. This means getting your hair cut if it is starting to look ragged and trimming your beard if you have one. Get out your best clothes and comb your hair. You've heard it said that you never get a second chance to make a first impression. This holds especially true for bureaucrats when dealing with Western travelers. There is still some sour aftertaste in the mouths of many of these officials from the 1960s when Western hippies roamed the world looking for cheap drugs and hassle-free enclaves in which to enjoy them.

The last thing you want to do is get labeled an indigent, so dress appropriately and put on your best and most respectful manners.

Most of the bureaucracy you'll come across will be at embassies when you are going to apply for a visa, at border crossings, and when you are applying for an extension of your visa. You are bound to find more hassles when traveling in developing countries than in the developed West, but you need to be mentally prepared for any circumstance wherever you travel.

Always say that you have a mission in life; a direction and sense of purpose. Be it a student, a teacher, or a writer. Whatever. You will probably fill out more forms while on your travels than you ever have before, and every time you will be asked for an occupation. Your occupation defines you.

If you only plan to travel in Europe, you will probably not need visas if you are from a Western country. If you need a visa (find out before you get to the border to avoid being turned back) you will have to obtain it by applying at an embassy or consulate in a large city of another country, before arriving at your intended destination. If you need a visa, a single Schengen visa gives you access to Austria, Belgium, the Czech Republic, Denmark, Estonia, Finland, France, Germany Greece, Hungary, Iceland, Italy, Latvia, Lithuania, Luxemburg, Malta, the Netherlands, Norway, Poland, Portugal, Slovakia, Slovenia, Spain, Sweden, and Switzerland. A Type C Schengen can be valid for maximum ninety days during a period of 180 days. The visa's validity period, first possible day of entry, and the day you must leave the Schengen area are written on the visa sticker. A visa is generally granted for a single entry, although multiple-entry visas are available.

In most cases, border officials in Europe will not even stamp your passport—you will get stamped once going into the Schengen zone and again on your way out.

Members of the British Commonwealth call their foreign diplomatic missions within other Commonwealth countries "High Commissions" (for example, the Canadian diplomatic mission in Kenya is called the High Commission, but the one in Rwanda is an embassy).

You can get the addresses of embassies in most travel guides or from the tourist bureau. For example, if you are in Kenya, and plan to go to Tanzania, the tourist office in Nairobi can give the address and directions to the Tanzanian embassy.

When you apply for a visa at the embassies or consulates of the countries you plan to visit, remember to bring four or five photographs of yourself. These photos are a required part of your application, presumably so if you go missing they will know what you look like. Sometimes visas are issued on the spot, but usually they take a few days. Factor this allowance into your plans if you are in a rush for the border.

Visas usually must be used within three months of their issue, so plan carefully if you want to stay longer in any of the countries en route. I usually get two at a time and then head to the capital of the second country to get visas for the next place I plan to visit.

You present your visa at your port of entry and are issued another stamp in your passport. Some countries, especially in parts of Africa, require that you check in with the police or military in every town, where they give you more stamps in your passport. When you leave a country, you again must go through customs and immigration and are given an exit visa.

If you need an exit visa before you get to the border, make sure you can get it before going there. Most countries do let you leave when you show up at the border, but a few, notably Syria, have been known to send travelers back to the capital to get an exit visa (that happened to me).

When you arrive at a backwoods border post that does not see too much traffic (this also has happened to me), you will sometimes have to look for the immigration official. It will be easy to forget, especially if no one is there to enforce it. To avoid problems later, be sure to find the immigration office and have your passport stamped. If you cannot find one, ask the first policeman or soldier you see for directions. Explain that you've just arrived and need an entrance stamp.

Audacity and ingenuity

Quite often, when dealing with bureaucracies, you will need a great deal of audacity and ingenuity. Necessity is the mother of invention and bureaucracy the father of creativity. Be careful when straying beyond the rules. Some travelers are willing to take more risks than others. Examples of this are alterations in your passport to give yourself an extension or tampering with your currency forms. Both carry big risks.

Your creative talents will be needed when filling out forms, in particular when stating your occupation and your reason for visiting the country. If you are trying to get a visa for a country that has a reputation for rejecting applications, be imaginative. The worst they can do is reject the application.

In 1984, I applied for a visa for the Sudan. I knew they were in the midst of a civil war and had just declared martial law and that visas were next to impossible to get. At the Sudanese embassy in Cairo, I managed to talk my way into getting the forms by saying I was a student of anthropology and that I needed to visit some

Sudanese villages as part of my research. I received a visa for two months, which I later extended to a one-year resident permit when I found a job in Khartoum teaching English and American cultural orientation to Ethiopian refugees who had been accepted into a resettlement program to start a new life in America.

Patience in officialdom

The best way to deal with the slow wheels of bureaucracy is to be patiently persistent. Wherever you are, in whatever country, you will find it generally true that the more you rush things, the less you'll get done. Let the person you are dealing with know that you are serious in your quest but are willing to wait as long as it takes to get the job done. Be serious, but light-hearted.

In countries of warmer climates, the general rule when conducting business is to grease the axles with a lot of polite conversation, before getting to the point. Talk about the weather, whatever fruit is in season, ask about the family, sports (but not politics), then broach the subject of your visa, or whatever it is you are applying for. In Muslim countries always begin with *Asalam Alaykum* (Peace be upon you) with the response *Wa alaykum wa salaam*.

As a last resort, take out that book you've been trying to finish and make yourself comfortable.

Busted

Hopefully this will not happen to you while abroad. First off, you should not be doing anything that could possibly be construed as illegal. The Midnight Express was no joke. Billy Hayes, the American depicted in the book and subsequent film, was lucky to get out of prison and escape from Turkey alive, but people may disagree on whether or not he got what he deserved. The condition of life in foreign prisons is well known, and if you are willing to take a chance by strapping chunks of hashish under your arms, then you must face the consequences of getting caught.

There are many Americans, Canadians, and Europeans in Turkish, Thai, and Peruvian prisons, and in just about every other country as well. You can visit these people, and I encourage you to do so. Most of them have long since realized their mistakes, but unfortunately still have several years to regret it. If you go to visit them, bring books and fresh fruit for them.

When traveling in unstable areas, you also must be aware of any behavior that might be misunderstood by local authorities. This includes photographing bridges, airports, or train stations.

If you are questioned by someone of authority, whether an officer in uniform or a 16-year-old boy with an AK47 machine gun at a roadblock, keep your cool. Smile a lot, make polite requests rather than demands, and sincerely compliment their country. Do everything you can to establish a good rapport and keep the conversation flowing.

Avoid writing anything political in your journals when traveling in volatile areas. If you absolutely must, write it in another language if you can (one that is not spoken in the country), and send it out in a letter home every chance you get. Don't leave anything in your pack that could get you into trouble, such as an Israeli address while traveling in Syria (yes, this happened to me too).

Stay well informed of current political situations in all areas you are traveling in. Know what you are getting yourself into if you plan on traveling in areas of conflict, and watch your every step while there.

16:

Avoiding Trouble

"The only aspect of our travels that is guaranteed to hold an audience is disaster."

— *Martha Gellhorn*

To avoid trouble while traveling, always err on the side of caution.

I had just spent the day exploring the ruins of an ancient Crusader castle on the Syrian side of the border with Lebanon. I arrived back in Homs long after dark and was walking to a house in the suburbs that served as the headquarters for the local chapter of the boy scouts of Syria.

The date was December 4, 1983 and something had just happened that day while I was exploring the ruins: Robert O. Goodman, a U.S. Navy navigator-bombardier, was shot down over Syrian positions in Lebanon and hauled to a military prison in Damascus. Had I kept up with news in the region, I would have known that Lebanon was in the throes of a brutal sectarian war and that U.S. forces were part of a large multinational force that had arrived to help broker peace. But as time went on they were getting sucked into an open confrontation with Damascus. As I was setting out to hike the mountains on the border in search of the ancient Roman city, Goodman was preparing to drop 1,000 pound bombs on Syrian tanks and anti-aircraft in Lebanon's Bekaa Valley, close to the Syrian border, and not far from where I was exploring.

It was long after dark when I arrived at the local boy scouts headquarters in Homs where I had sought shelter. Waiting for me were three or four military vehicles, filled with what seemed like very anxious and angry soldiers. They yelled at me in Arabic, pointing to the opened back door of one of the jeeps. Without hesitation, I quickly got in. There were no seatbelts.

We drove for about half an hour until we reached what looked like a military base with a heavily guarded entrance and a high fence topped with barbed wire. Several search lights shot dancing beams of light across the dusty night sky.

When we finally reached a nondescript building that looked left over from the French occupation, my belongings and I were brought into a small room with a big desk. My backpack was placed on the desk and I was told to wait on the chair in front of it. Not long afterwards a tall, affable, high-ranking officer walked in and sat behind the desk.

"What is your name?"

I told him.

"What are you doing in Syria?"

I told him I was there to explore the country, and to learn about its amazing history and place in the world. I explained I was on a mission to keep going east until I ended up back in the West and to learn as much as I could about the family of humanity along the way. Et cetera, et cetera.

"Where will you go after Syria?"

I explained my plan was to travel to Jordan.

"And then where?"

I explained from Jordan I would travel to Egypt, by way of Aqaba.

"You have no plans to travel to Israel?"

Of course not, I knew Syria was at war with Israel and it would not be a good idea to admit that I was on my way to Jerusalem and Bethlehem for Christmas. The officer and his men continued to inspect every nook and cranny of my backpack, going through every item carefully and reading every page of my journal untilthey found a small note that an Argentine friend I had met at the Youth

Hostel in Athens had left me. It was tucked into the back of my journal and said:

"When you get to Jerusalem, contact me at this number."

To make a long story short, they became very angry and suspicious and had only one question they kept repeating again and again and again, with a most graphic threat of torture that still makes me shudder when I think of it thirty-five years later:

"We only want to know whether you are Mossad or CIA."

I tried explaining that I did not lie, that I was not traveling to Israel but to "occupied Palestine" on *haj*, and that torture could not bring out anything else than the truth I was saying.

"Haj? You are going on pilgrimage?"

Yes, I explained, "Haj almasihiiyn." Almasihiiyn is the word Muslims use for Christians. It means "The followers of the Messiah." I had hoped, that as Muslims also accept Jesus as the Messiah, that this would appeal to a better side of my interrogators than the one that was beginning to emerge.

It worked, eventually. I was held in a cell while they decided what to do with me or received orders from higher up, probably Damascus. The next day I was released, and returned to the room I had rented. Once there, the local scout leaders were watching the news – and on it I learned of what had happened elsewhere in Syria that day. I later learned what happened to the Navy pilot: He was held for 30 days, treated well, and picked up in Damascus by Reverend Jessie Jackson.

Prepare

To avoid trouble while traveling, always err on the side of caution. With care, a sharpened awareness and a few simple caveats, hassles can be kept to a minimum. I will outline a few of my own insights here, but keep in mind your best protection will always be your intuition. If you sense something may not be right, back up and evaluate.

Scan all important documents, including your passport, any credit cards, and your international driver's license. I recommend all of this goes to a secure online site such as SecureSafe (www.secure-safe.com). You can also give them (or send via email) to someone you trust, like your mother. If everything somehow manages to get lost or stolen, it will be much easier to get them replaced if you have copies of everything somewhere safe.

Many things Westerners would consider unlikely to be stolen may be prized treasures abroad. Take care in choosing what you want to bring. Jewelry, watches, and electronic gadgetry such as an iPad or iPhone will not only make you vulnerable to theft but will be a pain to take care of and worry about. Wear a cheap drugstore watch if you can't do without one. Unless you really need it, leave the iPad at home and use a cyber cafe to catch up on email.

Most crimes against foreigners abroad are subtle and happen when the victim is caught unaware. The best way to lose something is to leave it unguarded even for a moment. Most possessions are lost by travelers when they leave them on a table and turn for "just a second." When this happens, someone who would not normally think of stealing anything from you is tempted, just a bit too much. When someone gets a chance to grab something that is worth more than he makes in a month or a year, he may go for it (yes, this has happened to me).

To minimize your chance of getting ripped off, make sure all your valuable possessions are in contact somewhere with your body. Get used to the sensation of having those things that are most important to you touching you somewhere. This is especially true for your money, cards, airline ticket, and passport.

In some cases, it may be wise to get a money belt that fits inside your pants. Always make sure you have enough small change and bills in your front pocket when you head out for the day, so that you won't have to dig in your pants for cash, letting all those in the area see where you put your money.

Look confident and as local as possible

One of the first things you'll learn when you go abroad for the first time, especially in developing countries, is that everyone, somehow, knows that you are a new arrival. You will be accosted by every beggar, panhandler, and con artist in the city. However, when you learn to make it look like you've lived there half your life, you will find yourself being left alone much more (but not entirely). When you walk down the street of a city you've arrived in for the first time, look calm and confident. Take in the scenery, but not with obvious

When you walk down the street of a city you've arrived in for the first time, look calm and confident.

awe or disbelief. Never take out a map in the middle of the street or sidewalk—go into a café, order a coffee, and then get yourself oriented by looking at your map.

Try and look as local as possible, regardless of the color of your skin. One thing I always do is buy a newspaper, ruffle it up, and carry it under my arm—even if it is in a language with characters I can't read, like Chinese or Korean. You'll be surprised at the difference this small gesture can make. Most targets of crime are targets precisely because the attackers know they are alone and without any local connections. If they are unsure who you might know locally, they are less inclined to take the risk or ripping you off.

At a restaurant, keep your bag on your lap, or at the very least right next to you with the strap running over your leg. Often, even the brightest and most seasoned of travelers will absent-mindedly leave a bag on a chair in a restaurant or a watch on a bathroom sink.

Armies of young kids around the world from Rome to Rio are well-trained in the art of ripping off foreigners. Often, they are so good, you won't even know you've been victimized until you get back to your hotel or reach into your pocket and find that your money has disappeared out a hole neatly cut through your pants. When walking around, keep your handbag closed at all times, and directly in front of you.

If you can't shake the habit of carrying a wallet, keep it in your front pocket. When you arrive in a city with your backpack, and must walk through crowded streets, be extra cautious of anyone approaching you from behind. Better yet, carry your pack in front of you.

It is always sad to lose something like a camera, especially one that is full of pictures from a day's exploring. I have gone through four of them, each lost for a stupid reason. But from each I learned. Keep it next to you always.

However, even with these precautions, something can happen. Once in Barcelona, while on an official trip for work, I was strolling confidently down the street when a man who I thought was drunk staggered up to me and asked me about my favorite football team. When I told him I was from Geneva, he started kicking around my feet asking me how they kick the ball in Switzerland. The entire encounter lasted no less than two or three minutes. I excused myself and continued walking towards my hotel. A few minutes later I thought to make a telephone call and reached into my pocket for my iPhone. It was gone.

Airplanes

Since the disastrous events of September 11, 2001 when terrorists hijacked airplanes and used them as weapons to bring down the World Trade Center in New York, many countries have implemented regulations against putting locks on your suitcase when checking it in for a flight. This means you must bring with you anything of value in your carry-on. Some countries do allow you to lock your baggage, and even have services at the airport to wrap your suitcase in plastic like a side of beef. Take advantage of this if you want to ensure that the same contents you packed make it all the way to your destination.

Hotels

To avoid tempting hotel cleaning staff with an addition to their wages, I always try to keep all my possessions organized and kept enclosed in my baggage, and the valuables locked in the safe. If you are staying in a hostel or a hotel without a safe, you can ask at the reception if a safe is available, and you can sign a receipt for the cash or valuables, passport, etc. that you keep there.

Walking down the street

Be aware of any attempts to distract your attention. There are thousands of ways thieves do this, and they are figuring out new ones all the time. Be constantly on the lookout for strange behavior, a commotion, or someone bumping into you. A favorite in South America is a form of condiment warfare, except instead of mustard gas, they've taken to just plain mustard.

One person will splatter you with mustard, while another looks up to the sky as if it were a bird, a plane or superman that dumped it on you. When you set your backpack or handbag down to clean yourself off, two others distract your attention further while the first one takes off with your gear. This unfortunately happened to me in Rio de Janeiro in 1992 at the Earth Summit. I had just come from photographing a session with the Dalai Lama and lost my camera

Be aware of con men when you are traveling, but don't keep your guard up too high or you may miss some valuable opportunities to engage with the locals.

and a full roll of film. Good thing I had just heard the Tibetan leader speak about letting go, non-attachment and the principles of impermanence. This story actually has a bright silver lining: After the incident I went to the offices of the United Nations Department of Public Information, where I was loaned a camera and met Pragati Pascale, who was instrumental when I later wrote a book on the Earth Summit called *A Planetary Reckoning*. She became an invaluable professional contact at the UN during my career there as well as a good friend.

Big cities around the world are alike in that they attract both the best and the worst of what a country has to offer. In urban areas, avoid the slums unless you are there for a reason. If you do go, bring nothing of value and leave your money belt in a safe. In big cities at night, travel by taxi or stay in the city center. When in a car of any kind, lock the doors for extra precaution, whether you are in Rome or Cairo. It is not uncommon for a thief to hop in the car when you are at a traffic light. I've heard stories of thieves throwing what appear to be poisonous snakes into the car so that when the driver jumps out, the thief pulls the snake out with a stick and drives off with the car.

Avoiding violent crime

Try to avoid places without people in the city and those with too many people. You can be held up in alleys or stairways with no witnesses around. In crowds, you are vulnerable to pickpockets and bag-slashers (groups of young boys who slash your bag or back pocket with a razor blade and steal the contents).

Unless you are in a secured area, avoid going to the beach with any valuables, not even a watch. Go with just your bathing suit and a towel. If you want to photograph the beach, go with friends. There are exceptions to this of course, especially if you are on a secluded island. But if you are near a city like Rio de Janeiro, Mumbai, or even Los Angeles, be careful.

If you are confronted anywhere, give the assailant what he wants. Chances are you are carrying more with you than either he or any of his friends could dream of possessing unless they steal it from you. It's nothing personal: they want what you have and are willing to do anything for it—including possibly taking your life.

Be sure to have a little cash with you that you can give to a thief in case you are robbed. Thugs often get upset and can be violent if you have nothing to give them.

I have developed the habit of carrying a mock wallet in my back pocket, with a couple of expired credit cards and a bunch of small bills. I even did this while living in Switzerland. Keep your real valuables, credit cards, ID cards etc. in your money belt and/or in a small wallet in your front pocket. If you are robbed, be polite and give up your wallet from your back pocket. The assailant should be content and leave you alone (unless he has read this book).

Don't let this scare you away from travel. Horror stories are a dime a dozen on the road and are only meant to educate you, not frighten you or make you paranoid. There are risks to living, and the fewer you take, the less you gain. The reason so few people get out and enjoy life is because they are afraid that something bad will happen. Stay aware but keep a positive attitude. Negative emotions and attitudes only bring on negative manifestations. There is a metaphysical truth to be said about the influence thinking has on the reality one experiences. Stay positive, have faith, and pay attention to details. As the Arabs say: "Trust in Allah but tie your camel."

Con men

Con men have been around since the dawn of humankind, and in each country they have their own favorite schemes. Keep in touch with the traveler's grapevine to find out what they are up to in your area. Some can be quite harmless if you fall prey to their deceptions, and the most you'll lose is some money. Others will take you for everything you've got, including your life.

In the Philippines, there are (or used to be) two common con practices: The first is to get an unsuspecting foreigner to talk about gambling. The con man then slyly informs you that he has a friend who works in the gambling casino and that a very rich client is coming over to play. They need one more "smart" person to deal a third hand, and it would look more realistic if that person was a Westerner.

They get you in the door and the show begins. The rich man comes dressed in a tuxedo and fancy jewelry. You start to play, and he begins to lose. You've got a stack of money in front of you and it looks really good. Then the tables turn, and you start losing. You lose and lose, until all the money that was given to you goes to the rich man (is there any wonder why he's so rich?). Then the pressure is put on, and you are asked to put some of your own money up. I knew a guy who even went with his new friends to the bank so he could get money off his credit card! It sounds ridiculous, but unsuspecting travelers do fall prey to such practices.

Another con approach is a lot simpler but much more danger-ous. You are approached by one or two people of your own age who make friends with you. They invite you to their house for a cup of coffee or perhaps a soft drink, and when you get there they give you a drink heavily laden with a chemical to knock you out. While you are unconscious, they strip you of all your valuables and dump you on the side of the street somewhere. These guys are con artists, not chemists, and could easily give you an overdose. I have even heard of women in Pattaya who put a knock-out drug on their breasts so that when a man kisses them he quickly passes out, only to wake up the next day without clothes or money.

To avoid con men, keep your guard up, but not high enough so that you will screen out those locals who are honestly sincere in wanting to meet you. Look steadily at their eyes, and see if they twitch. Are they bloodshot? Do they emanate calm kindness or stress? Watch for nervous tendencies, then trust your gut-level instinct. If you have even the slightest doubt, don't trust them. Be nice, but firm in your response to them. Usually a simple but firm "no" should suffice. Walk away calmly.

Finding yourself on the wrong side of the law

There is no excuse for consciously breaking the law anywhere. In simple terms: Know what the law is and don't break it. By breaking the law, you will realize the naked truth of the maxim "When in Rome do as the Romans." When the locals break the law, they go to jail, when a foreigner breaks a law, he goes to jail. Very rarely are there any exceptions. Sometimes the crimes can be seemingly innocuous: In 2007, Oliver Jufer of Switzerland was sentenced to ten years in jail in Thailand for defacing images of King Bhumibok Adulyadej with a can of spray paint. Ignorance is rarely a defense in a court of law.

Drugs

In some places you will find that the attitude about drugs is quite liberal. In India they even sell hash from government outlets and the local cafés sell yogurt drinks mixed with hashish. If you choose to partake in this aspect of the local culture, be careful. Doing drugs will automatically make you suspect of all kinds of nefarious crimes, and it can give the local police an excuse to throw you in prison in hopes of extracting a bribe.

Not only does doing drugs put you at an incredible risk of being forced into an efficient language school (after ten years or so in a local jail you should be able to speak the local language rather fluently), but it also hampers your judgment and impairs your perception. When you are high, you run a greater risk of getting ripped off, getting lost and wandering into a dangerous neighborhood, or burning out and losing all contact with your surroundings. It is not uncommon for Westerners to completely lose their minds when on drugs in a foreign country, and end up forgotten about for years in a filthy mental institution. You can also get addicted and throw your life away for that "one last hit." India and Pakistan are full of Westerners who have sold their possessions and passports and beg from other Westerners, so they can buy that extra bit of opium.

But I'm innocent!

It was 1984 and I had just spent three weeks—twenty-one days and twenty-one nights—on a slow barge traveling up the Nile River in Sudan from Kosti to Juba. When I finally arrived in the southern capital, I was promptly arrested and had all my possessions taken.

I was held for three weeks while the authorities waited for instructions from Khartoum. Eventually I was released and escorted to the Uganda border at Nimule, without my film or notebooks.

—

Occasionally, travelers may find themselves in trouble with the law when there is nothing they did to deserve it. The most common of these is being accused of spying. To avoid this, avoid all suspicious behavior, including taking pictures of bridges, train stations, or soldiers. Don't carry stuff with you that could be considered subversive material.

Avoid all suspicious behavior, including taking pictures of border crossings.

When traveling in politically unstable areas, don't wear military fatigues. Do not accept packages from anyone to carry for them and be careful when crossing borders that someone doesn't slip something in your bag for you to unknowingly smuggle.

Write home or to a friend as often as possible, especially when traveling in politically volatile areas, or be sure to update your travel blog regularly. This way, if you disappear, it will be easier to track you down.

If you do find yourself in jail, get word to your embassy via any means possible. The "one phone call" tradition is not internationally recognized so you may have to be creative. Stay calm and relaxed. Try to diffuse the situation through a bit of humor and by appealing to their senses and religious sentiments.

Explain that you are a traveler, a philosopher, a lover of life, and a student. Tell them you came to their country because you heard their people were the friendliest in the entire region. Declare your innocence and maintain faith that in the end they will see that you are, in fact, innocent.

The black market

The black market, also known as the parallel market, is not as nefarious as it sounds. For the most part, there are no cloak-and-dagger types, high adventure in mysterious back-alleys, or risk of life.

But there are other risks. The black market is illegal in most countries (even though many government officials deal regularly in it), and you could get cheated (or worse, arrested) if you are not careful.

There are advantages to the black market. In Tanzania, for example, a U.S. dollar in the bank brought sixteen shillings in 1985. In the parallel market however, one could get 130 (the Tanzanian government has since relaxed its hold on the economy and the black market has all but disappeared).

Economists call such a system a "dual economy," which arises naturally when the marketplace puts too many constraints on financial transactions. When governments attempt to circumvent market economies by regulating what will be traded and at what prices, the supply and demand principle is merely suppressed. Like hydraulic fluid, it pushes up in other areas. For example, by restricting the importation of foreign truck parts, the mechanics are left with no alternative but to look to unofficial sources for supply.

Wherever there is demand, supply materializes, usually in the form of someone smuggling in the needed parts from a neighboring country. This "smuggling entrepreneur" will obviously need hard currency for his labor so he can return and buy more truck parts. He thus demands payment in American dollars or another 'hard' currency (one

Following a few simple caveats should ensure your travel experience is a good one.

that can be readily traded on world markets). The truck driver must buy his dollars directly from a tourist or from a "middle man" (of which there are many) who takes a cut for his involvement.

The more restrictions the government imposes on such imports, the more of a demand there will be for the dollars or other hard currencies, which are not in great supply. The resulting equation pushes the price of the dollar much higher than what the government offers.

In the 1980s, many governments reacted to the dual economy by regulating everything. This meant that travelers had to declare their currency upon entering the country, and then get official records of transactions from the bank when you change your money "officially." Upon leaving the country, the immigration officials checked their currency declaration forms to see that bank slips plus remaining cash equaled the amount originally declared.

Some travelers exchange their currency on the dual market to take advantage of the higher exchange rate. If you choose to do this, be aware that you are on your own. Know the consequences and possible risks.

Bribing

Paying an extra gratuity for services to be rendered is like giving a tip in advance, and goes by a variety of euphemisms from "buying tea" to baksheesh. The places where this happens could be anywhere from the post office to the airline office to the immigration office.

You may find that in places with weak governance structures where public servants often aren't paid a living wage, corruption is what makes things function. It is also a cancer that hinders a society and often rewards the worst people and agendas. That said, my advice is not to engage in or encourage any form of bribing, unless you are in a corner and see no way out.

17:

Staying Healthy

"A wise man ought to realize
that health is his most valuable possession
and learn how to treat his illnesses
by his own judgment."

— *Hippocrates*

Staying healthy means eating right and taking good care or yourself.

Before leaving on your journey, consider getting into top physical shape. If you are not already at your peak performance, consider walking a mile or two daily, a few months before your departure. Spend time at the gym and work on your cardiovascular exercise to improve stamina. Travel can be exhausting, and the shape you are in before you leave will make a world of difference healthwise while you are on the road.

When traveling abroad, especially in lesser-developed countries, always pay attention to your health. You are under enough pressure from the normal stress of traveling and what you do not need is a debilitating illness. Nothing can ruin your trip faster than a simple toothache, an attack of diarrhea, or any number of illnesses you can get while on the road.

There are some bugs that are hard to avoid when traveling in lesser-developed countries, but most of these are minor illnesses. If you are careful, are in good health, wash your hands regularly, and use hand sanitizer, you can minimize your risk significantly.

This chapter is not meant to replace sound medical advice. It is offered by way of a general overview of what to think of in terms of staying healthy. If at all in doubt about a medical situation you may find yourself in while traveling, see a doctor immediately.

When you are feeling run down, do not push yourself. Often all you need is a good rest. Traveling can be extremely taxing physically. Rather than letting yourself fall ill, it is better to take a few days chilling out: Get yourself a comfortable room and sleep.

The first rule in avoiding illnesses is the same no matter where you are, how old you are, or what you are doing—staying healthy means eating right and taking good care or yourself.

Eating right

A long time ago Hippocrates said, "let food be your medicine." If we want to stay healthy, we need to eat well. Take care of your body and your body will take care of you. The key to healthy eating and staying strong when traveling is to enjoy a variety of nutritious foods from each of the 5 food groups:

» Fruit: fruit provides vitamins, minerals, dietary fibre and many phytonutrients (nutrients naturally present in plants), that your body needs to stay healthy.

» Grain (cereal) foods: if possible, try to find wholegrain and/or high fibre varieties of bread, cereals, rice, pasta, noodles, etc. Refined grain products such as white bread can be high in added sugar, fat, and sodium.

» Lean meats and poultry, fish, eggs, tofu, nuts and seeds and legumes/beans: our bodies use protein to produce specialized chemicals such as hemoglobin and adrenalin. Protein also builds, maintains, and repairs the tissues in our body.

» Vegetables and legumes/beans: vegetables should make up a large part of your daily food intake. They provide vitamins, minerals, dietary fiber and phytonutrients to help your body stay healthy.

Vitamin C helps reinforce the body's immune system so eat foods with a high vitamin C content like garlic and citrus. If you don't think you'll be able to get enough from natural sources, bring a supplement in pill form as well as a good supply of multi-vitamins. Leave the vitamins in their original containers so border officials won't arrest you on suspicion of carrying illegal drugs.

Any discomfort in your digestive system should be dealt with quickly, carefully, and appropriately. If the digestive system isn't working properly, your body won't be able to go about its everyday activities. To maintain a regular supply of fuel, your digestive system must be in good shape. Common problems in the digestive tract are constipation, diarrhea, ulcers, reflux disease, and parasitic infestations. All these conditions result in pain, discomfort, and inflammation. If the digestive disorders and infestations are not taken care of, you will suffer from deficiencies which could impede the rest of your organs—causing them to gradually shut down because the necessary nutrients are not being properly assimilated.

There are many medicines for digestive problems and infestations available at pharmacies worldwide. However, many people still prefer to use the simple, yet effective remedies that are natural, such as everyday garlic. If the DIY approach does not work after a few days, do not hesitate to see a doctor.

Garlic—not just for vampires
Garlic has been used as a natural remedy to combat numerous ailments since the beginning of recorded history. Those in the know continue to use it in alternative medicines as a natural, organic solution to many diseases and medical conditions because of its antibacterial, anti-inflammatory, and anti-parasitic properties. Garlic can target colitis, diarrhea, dysentery, and parasitic infestations. The best part is that it does not negatively affect the good bacteria

and flora that the digestive system needs to perform its duties. Garlic only affects the bad organisms, so the gastrointestinal tract can be rebalanced and return you to good health. Thus, to maintain good digestive health, include garlic in your daily diet—at home and when traveling.

Medical and dental checkups

Visit your physician before you depart to get a full medical examination and have your teeth cleaned and polished. The last thing you want is to fall ill after arriving in a foreign country or suffer from an excruciating toothache. Tell your doctor where you plan to go and discuss the preventions and treatments of common ailments that are associated with international travel.

Garlic has been used as a natural remedy to combat numerous ailments since the beginning of recorded history.

Travelers who require regular prescription medicines should carry a double supply. Put one in your carry-on luggage and one in your suitcase/backpack. Get a letter from your doctor describing the medicine and what it is used for. Prescriptions from your doctor are not necessarily valid abroad, but drugs that are sold only through prescription in the United States are often sold over-the-counter overseas. Keep a copy of your prescription in your SecureSafe vault, mentioned earlier.

If you need to see a doctor or a dentist while in a foreign country, your embassy will give you a list of recommended physicians and dentists. Some on the list will have been trained in the United States or Europe and, if they are recommended by a U.S. embassy, they should speak English.

Immunizations

One of the most welcome miracles of modern medicine is the ability to prevent many otherwise deadly diseases through immunization. Appropriate immunizations increase the safety margin of traveling in many regions of the world and are a prerequisite to entering some countries (for example, most countries in East Africa require a yellow fever vaccination certificate to gain entry). Most required vaccinations are for cholera and yellow fever, but it is a good idea to make sure you are up on tetanus and measles. To minimize your risk of getting hepatitis, get gamma globulin shots. Ask your physician which vaccinations you will need to get, or check this web page at the World Health Organization website: www.who.int/topics/vaccines/en/

You will need to record your vaccinations in an International Certificate of Vaccinations, which is a small yellow pamphlet that you will have to guard as securely as you guard your passport. Get one from your doctor before you go. Like a passport, this pamphlet will be requested at most border crossings and immigration check points. You will need to know what immunizations are required for the countries you plan to visit, and it is advisable to get them before you go. If you are on the road when your vaccinations expire, go to a reputable clinic or ask at your embassy where you can get them updated.

There are many illnesses in the world today, but far fewer than there were a hundred years ago. The following list outlines what the greatest threats to the traveler are and how to avoid them.

Health risks to watch out for when traveling

The primary reason I put this section in Chapter 18 is that on the surface the following could scare you off from traveling. If you travel long enough, you are bound to get sick – if you stay at home long enough, you are bound to get sick. For me, getting sick is just part of life; you can minimize it through taking basic precautions, but sooner or later the bugs will catch up with you.

Animals

A February 2018 article in *Science Alert* ranks the world's fifteen deadliest animals—all of which you should watch out for in your travels. Most of the deaths caused by animals, according to the report, have less to do with the animals themselves than the diseases they unwittingly transmit. You may be surprised by some in the list—I know I was.

At the bottom of the list are sharks, killing only about six people a year. Next on the list are wolves, which take ten unlucky lives each year, and then lions—which attack and kill twenty-two people per year.

This is where the numbers start to climb rapidly. A 2005 National Geographic article said that 500 people a year are killed in elephant attacks, while hippos—renowned vegetarians—kill another 500. Crocodiles, while definitely not vegetarians, eat more than 1,000 people annually.

Moving now to parasites, the tapeworm is responsible for an infection called cysticercosis that kills an estimated 700 people a year. The Ascaris roundworm leads to an infection called ascariasis that kills an estimated 4,500 people a year—mostly kids.

Watch out for the tsetse, sometimes spelled tzetze and also known as tik-tik flies. These are large biting flies that inhabit much of tropical Africa. These dangerous little beasts transmit a disease called sleeping sickness, a parasitic infection that at first can lead to headaches, fever, joint pain, and itchiness, but later can lead to some serious neurological problems. The number of deaths has been decreasing, but these little buggers still kill about 10,000 people a year.

The assassin bug, also called the kissing bug, is responsible for carrying Chagas disease, which kills about 12,000 people a year on average—for whom the kissing bug brings the kiss of death.

Next up the list is the freshwater snail, which carries parasitic worms that infect people with a disease called schistosomiasis that can cause intense abdominal pain and blood in the stool or urine, killing anywhere between 20,000 and 200,000 people each year, according to the World Health Organization.

Dogs are probably the greatest worry—they kill about 35,000 people annually through the transmission of rabies. If they are going to attack you at all, they are most likely to do so at night when packs often roam the streets looking for something to eat. If you run into one that doesn't appear to be friendly, grab the nearest rock to protect yourself. If there isn't one, simply reach for the ground as if picking up a rock. Dogs around the world have been conditioned to run when a human reaches for a rock. In some cities it is also good to carry a walking stick, especially if you need to walk through dark streets.

Snakes, which have been menacing humans since the Garden of Eden, kill more than 100,000 people a year. Worse still, there's a troubling shortage of an essential antivenom. Although snakes kill a lot of people, a much more dangerous animal (and one which is much more difficult to avoid) is the human. According to the United Nations Office on Drugs and Crime (UNODC), there were about 437,000 homicides in 2012 (the last year a full, complete assessment was undertaken), making humans the second most deadly animal (and the deadliest mammal) to humans.

This now brings us to number one, the deadliest of all creatures on this planet, which kills more humans than any other: the mosquito. There are more about 3,500 species of mosquito throughout the world, about 170 species in the United States alone. Only female mosquitoes feed on blood, which they need to produce eggs. Male mosquitoes do not bite, preferring the nectar of flowers.

Mosquitos kill more than 750,000 people each year. That's three quarters of a million lives lost to the pesky little insects. Malaria by itself is responsible for more than half of mosquito-related deaths, predominantly in sub-Saharan Africa. The good news is malaria is on the decline: The incidence of malaria fell by thirty-seven percent between 2000 and 2015. Dengue fever, which also is transmitted by mosquitos, has become a leading cause of hospitalization and death among children in Latin-America and a few Asian countries.

Hepatitis

By far the most common horror story of ruined travels from people returning from abroad is hepatitis, a viral infection of the liver. It is common in places like India and parts of Africa and South America where the sanitary conditions are less than ideal. There are different types of hepatitis, with the most common being a form known as infectious hepatitis, or simply "hepatitis A." Worldwide in 2015, hepatitis A occurred in about 114 million people, chronic hepatitis B affected about 343 million people, and chronic hepatitis C about 142 million people.

Hepatitis A is usually spread by a virus in contaminated food and water. Its symptoms are fever, jaundice (when your skin turns yellow), fatigue, nausea, and intense stomach pain (not a pretty picture). Since there is no specific treatment other than riding out the storm (which can take months). Prevention of hepatitis is very important. The importance of taking precautions in what you eat and drink cannot be over emphasized. In unsanitary environments, stay away from unpeeled fruit and vegetables, water, and ice.

If you think you may be at risk of exposure to hepatitis, get vaccinated.

Cholera

Cholera, which is caused by eating or drinking contaminated food or water, causes severe diarrhea and dehydration. Outbreaks of this disease usually occur in very poor sanitary conditions. Many countries require immunization for cholera, but shots are only good for six months. For effective immunization, you need to get two shots, both of which are deep and slightly painful.

However, if you are sure you will not be dining in slums or otherwise be in danger of contacting cholera, a lighter shot will fill the requirement. This is usually the one taken by travelers.

Dengue fever

There are no completely safe preventatives for this mosquito-spread disease, other than avoiding getting bitten. The first symptoms are an onset of fever, headaches, and joint and muscle pains followed by a rash. Serious complications are not common, but if you experience any of these symptoms, contact a doctor immediately.

Sleeping sickness

In some areas of tropical Africa, tsetse flies, which are twice the size of a housefly, carry this disease. Sleeping sickness is also known as trypanosomiasis. There is no known immunization, so avoid being bitten when traveling in tropical Africa. Use a strong insect repellent with DEET. The flies are attracted to large moving objects like buses and to aftershave and dark colors. Swelling at the site of the bite about five days later is followed by fever within a week or two. If you experience this, contact a doctor, though the symptoms sound serious, it is usually cured quickly through prompt medical attention.

Yellow fever

Yellow fever is spread through the inadvertent and seemingly innocent activities of the mosquito, which transmits a virus that attacks the liver and other organs. It is common in parts of Africa and South America, where most countries require immunization for entry.

Yellow fever causes jaundice and brings on high fever and bleeding problems. The degrees of symptoms range from mild illness to death. In recent years, much has been done to eradicate this sickness, though there is still a slight risk of contracting it if the traveler is not properly vaccinated. Yellow fever vaccinations are usually good for ten years.

Bilharzia

It's over 100 degrees outside with ninety-five percent humidity. The lake looks so cool and inviting. Just a quick dip to cool off, but not so fast. It may look clean, but like many lakes in tropical regions today it could be infected with the schistosoma parasite, a small worm that burrows into your skin and makes a home in your intestines and liver.

The result is an illness called schistosomiasis, also known as bilharzia. Fortunately, most cases are caused only by prolonged and frequent contact with infected water. Casual exposure is very unlikely to make you sick, but it is best to be careful. Bilharzia is most common in areas with stagnant water and is not found in rivers or streams. There is more bilharzia in Africa than other places in the world. It doesn't exist in salt water.

Malaria

Malaria death rates have fallen by more than sixty percent worldwide since the year 2000. Progress has been made possible, in large part, through the wide-scale deployment of effective vector control tools that target malaria-carrying mosquitoes—primarily long-lasting insecticidal nets (LLINs) and also indoor residual spraying (IRS).

However, there were still 216 million malaria cases worldwide in 2016 with 445,000 of these cases ending in death. To avoid malaria, a traveler, in preparing for the journey, needs to be aware of exactly what malaria is, how to prevent it, and the methods for curing it. I have had malaria several times in very remote areas and without access to medical care. The advice in this section, received from several sources, probably saved my life. I now pass it on to you.

An unsuspecting agent of destruction, the female mosquito is just looking after the best interests of her unborn young. The female mosquito pierces the skin of someone who is sick with malaria to get blood for her eggs, taking with her the parasite that is in the bloodstream.

When the mosquito flies back to her nest of eggs, showering them with your blood, she retains with her the parasites. She then carries them to the next person she lands on to extract more blood. After getting her second fill for the day, she, like all mosquitoes, leaves behind a natural disinfectant in the skin to prevent infection, depositing the parasites at the same time. It is this seemingly benevolent action that spreads one of the world's deadliest illnesses.

The parasites, overjoyed at being in a fresh environment, head straight for the liver to relax and reinforce their ranks preparing for battle. Reproducing asexually in the liver's cells, they increase their numbers, taking anywhere from two to six weeks to incubate. When the time is right, the newly formed battalions of parasites dig themselves in and wait.

It is only when the body's defenses are down that these vicious foes to humankind release their fury. Having multiplied beyond capacity, they burst out into the bloodstream, entering the red blood cells and wreaking general havoc on the entire system.

The parasites feed on the hemoglobin in the cells, entering them and reproducing further until the cells explode, releasing more parasites into the bloodstream. On the outside, the victim suffers intense headaches, constricting muscles, weakness, an enlarged spleen, alternating high fever, and chills. The malarial fever has begun.

To avoid malaria, know where you are going and find out from a qualified tropical diseases clinic which strains of malaria are most prominent there. You will need to take with you a supply of preventative medicine known as a prophylaxis. Be sure to take more than enough to last through your trip in the region. Most types of medicine require that you begin your dosage a few weeks before entering malaria territory.

The pills generally come in two categories: weekly or daily. Most people prefer the weekly ones because they are easiest to remember. Choose a day like Sunday, or one that you are not likely to forget. Highlight that day on the calendar in bright ink.

The only sure way to avoid contact with the malarial parasite is to avoid contact with the mosquito. Mosquitoes like to dine at about the same time you do so be sure to dress fully in the evening—especially if you are eating dinner in the open air. Sandals are indeed the most comfortable kind of footwear in the tropics, but the mosquito's favored delicacy is the ankle. Be sure to wear your socks. Avoid wearing dark colors, especially black, navy, and red. The Aedes aegypti mosquito which transmits Zika virus, dengue fever, and Chikungunya is attracted to red and black, so avoid that color combination at all costs.

Mosquitoes are very sensitive to scents produced when you sweat, such as ammonia, lactic acid, and uric acid. Thus, the more you perspire and the more it soaks into clothing (like socks or t-shirts) the more the more bacteria build up on your skin (especially if you're exercising or working outside and getting dirty), and the more mosquitoes will be attracted to you. Mosquitoes are also attracted by heat, meaning the bigger you are, the more attractive a buffet you become. Mosquitoes also love perfumes and colognes with a particular attraction to floral scents. They're also lured by skincare products that contain alpha-hydroxy acids.

Mosquitoes can detect carbon dioxide in the air and use that to track down their meals. Adults are especially attractive because they emit more carbon dioxide than children and pets.

If you must bare your skin, carry lots of repellent. There are numerous kinds of repellent on the shelves these days, but most are made for the lightweight North American mosquitoes, providing minimal protection in the tropics. Make sure the repellent has a high content of the chemical DEET (Diethyl O-Toluamide).

A mosquito net is another integral part of the antimalaria kit. While keeping the malaria at a safe distance, a good net will also ensure a good night's sleep, safe from swarming, obnoxious mosquitoes.

Dysentery and related belly problems

Probably the most common illness among travelers is diarrhea, often referred to as Delhi Belly or Montezuma's revenge. Whether you are going to Swaziland or Switzerland you will most likely be making the mad dash to the toilet sometime after your arrival. Don't panic. Diarrhea is a perfectly normal adjustment your body is making to its new environment. It is usually caused by a bacterium called Escherichia coli, also known as E. coli. Everyone without exception has a group of these guys living harmlessly in his or her colon. When you travel abroad you pick up a new kind of Escherichia coli (E. coli) that your system is not used to your body reacts with diarrhea. Aside from E. coli, there are other kinds of bacteria and parasites that can cause diarrhea, but usually the attacks are less frequent.

When you find yourself with a case of the runs, don't reach too quickly for that jar of anti-diarrhea pills. Doing this can lead to unwanted side effects: It prevents your body's self-sufficient immune system from building up resistance and the medicine can actually harm some of the good bacteria inside you that you need for the normal digestion of food. Give yourself a few days, and if you are not getting better, consider seeing a doctor or trying some of many anti-diarrhea pills you can get at almost any pharmacy. In most countries you can just show up at the pharmacy with a description of your ailment.

There are a few handy precautions to keep in mind that will minimize your risk of getting diarrhea. If you are in the tropics, eat a few papaya seeds every day. If you do get a case of the runs, try taking about eight to ten seeds. Yogurt helps a lot with its own bacteria, but avoid other kinds of dairy products. Sprinkle lime juice on your food to kill harmful bacteria. (This is how the lime craze got started with Mexican beer in the U.S. The Mexicans take the lime and wipe off the top of the bottle to kill any bacteria there. The gringos started dropping the lime in the bottle.)

Keep up your intake of Vitamin C through supplements or by eating lots of garlic and citrus. Avoid uncooked foods, unless they come in a natural wrapper (like a banana).

Two tablespoons of Pepto-Bismol a day can keep the diarrhea away. Slippery elm is an item available at most health food stores and can accomplish the same thing in a natural way. Take a teaspoon of this tan powder and stir it into a cup of warm water.

If you are cooking for yourself, clean everything well before eating it. Fruits and vegetables that cannot be peeled should be sterilized. Put them in a sink of water with seven to ten drops of iodine; this will kill any bacteria that could be harmful. Iodine can also be used in water with a few drops per liter, but water that is doubtful should be boiled for ten minutes, filtered, then purified with iodine or water purification product. In place of iodine, bleach is a good substitute. Use the same ratio as for iodine.

The toilets you may have to use when traveling abroad often leave much to be desired. To protect yourself from the unsanitary conditions, learn to squat. Most countries around the world have only squat toilets, but if it is the sit-down type, lift up the seat and squat anyway. Wash your hands after each call from Mother Nature.

Diarrhea can cause severe dehydration. Simply drinking bottled water and soft drinks is not enough. The following solution has been recommended by the World Health Organization as a diarrhea rehydration quick-fix: ¼ tablespoon potassium chloride, ½ teaspoon sodium bicarbonate, ½ teaspoon table salt, and 2 teaspoons of glucose or 4 teaspoons sucrose all added to one quart of water. If you cannot get the above ingredients the following two solutions also have been recommended: a glass of fruit juice mixed with a pinch of salt, ½ teaspoon honey and a teaspoon of sugar to help the medicine go down or a glass of water with ¼ teaspoon of baking soda. Avoid milk, coffee, strong tea, alcohol, and anything with caffeine when your stomach is giving you trouble.

If your diarrhea does not stop in forty-eight hours, or if you see blood mixed in with your stool, consult a doctor immediately. You do not want to take any chances if you think you might have amoebic dysentery, which means there may be some nasty little critters in your stomach. If this is the case, a doctor will need to take a stool sample to determine exactly what medicine you will need to treat whatever is inside you.

Sexually transmitted diseases

Although connecting and sharing intimacy with someone from another culture can offer amazing experiences and opportunities to learn and share, there are caveats that should be carefully considered.

Sexually transmitted diseases (STDs), also referred to as sexually transmitted infections (STIs) and venereal diseases (VD), are commonly spread by sex. Most cases initially do not cause any symptoms, which causes a greater risk of passing the disease on to others.

There are more than thirty different documented bacteria, viruses, and parasites which can cause STIs. Bacterial STIs include chlamydia, gonorrhea, and syphilis among others. Viral STIs include genital herpes, HIV/AIDS, and genital warts among others. While usually spread by sex, some STIs can also be spread by non-sexual contact with contaminated blood and tissues, breastfeeding, or during childbirth. STI diagnostic tests are easily available in the developed world, but this is often not the case in the developing world.

The solution for the health-conscious traveler? Travel with a significant other or do without. The chance of getting something is just as great from a fellow traveler met on the road as it is from a local, so exercise caution always. Some vaccinations may also decrease the risk of certain infections including hepatitis B and some types of HPV. Safer sex practices such as use of condoms, having a smaller number of sexual partners, and being in a relationship where each person only has sex with the other also decreases the risk.

You will notice that sex in some countries is practically taboo while in others it could be more accepted than you are used to. If you are traveling in the latter, especially in places like Thailand, Kenya, or Brazil, be aware of what you are doing. This advice is for men and women.

Carry a good supply of condoms if you think you might be active. In fact, always carry a six pack *just in case*—both men and women. Better to have and not need, than to need and not have. Do not, under any circumstances, take chances. All it takes is one evening of unprotected passion and you could get stuck with something you will remember for the rest of your possibly shortened life.

The sun
Only mad dogs and Englishmen, it is said, go out in the midday sun. In the West, many white people have a love affair with the golden tan, and this is often one of their reasons for traveling abroad. Many people find it embarrassing to come back from somewhere warm without a tan.

If you are white and traveling in tropical climates, it is good to have a tan to protect yourself from the harmful effects of the sun's intensity. But get it slowly. Remember that the sun may be stronger in many parts of the world than you are used to. Higher elevations are often cooler, but the sun is much more intense, especially with a thinning ozone layer. Until you get a solid tan, wear plenty of sunscreen.

The sun and heat are not to be taken lightly. Heat stroke, heat exhaustion, sunburn, and dehydration are all serious. Wear a hat, and drink plenty of liquids when visiting hot countries. When you sweat excessively, the body loses a lot of salt and severe cramps can result. When this happens, increase your intake of salt by salting your food more heavily than usual.

As with most travel-related symptoms, your body will go through an adjustment phase. Allowing your body to adjust gradually to changes in climate will solve most of the initial problems you experience. However, if you experience any abnormal symptoms for more than a few days, it is wise to see a local physician.

Cuts and superficial wounds

If you cut or scrape yourself, clean it, apply an antibacterial ointment, and cover it. At night, it is a good idea to let the wound breathe, but, if there is a lot of dust in the air, keep something over it. In the tropics, wounds can easily become infected. Even a seemingly innocent scrape can turn into a nightmare, especially coral scrapes if you dive or snorkel.

If you cut yourself deeply, immediately apply firm pressure, and be prepared to hold it there for up to an hour to stop the bleeding. If possible, raise the cut part of your body above the heart. If you have ice, use it with the pressure (the word "ice" is good to remember when dealing with lacerations—Ice, Compression, Elevation).

When you get the bleeding to stop, wash it gently with soap and apply a clean bandage.

Descriptions of travel medical care could easily turn into a first-aid manual. If you plan to be on the road for an extended period, it is advisable to get at least some rudimentary first aid training.

Jet lag

When you're flying across time zones, especially several of them, it can take your body awhile to adjust during which time you may suffer from fatigue, insomnia, constipation, diarrhea, confusion, and more. Fortunately, there are some effective things you can do to either prevent jet lag or to aid your recovery from jet lag once it sets in.

Before leaving, start to prepare yourself for the time shift. Every week, push your schedule one hour back or forward, depending on where you're going. I often stay up the night before, and then sleep on the plane (window seat!), using Ambien or another sleeping pill.

Drink a lot of water before, during, and after your long flight. Dehydration is one of the symptoms of jet lag and the dry, cabin air on the plane only dries you up more. If they are offering free drinks on the plane, decline them. While a triple scotch on the rocks may help you fall asleep on the plane, you'll wake up with a horrible hangover made worse by jetlag.

To help offset jet lag, move your watch ahead before you leave to mentally prepare yourself for the time change. When on the plane, sleep if it is nighttime at your destination; stay awake if it's daytime. Once you arrive at your destination, go for a walk to unwind and give your body some exercise. Don't push yourself. Get yourself some reading material and get plenty of rest.

The initial symptoms of the dreaded jet lag should wear off in a day or two. To help fall asleep at night, when you need sleep for energy the next day, try using melatonin. Melatonin is a natural hormone made by your body's pineal gland—a pea-sized node located just above the middle of the brain. During the day the pineal is inactive. When the sunsets, the pineal is "turned on" by the suprachiasmatic nucleus (SCN) in the eye (which perceives daylight) and begins to actively produce melatonin, which is released into the blood. Usually, this occurs around 9 p.m. As a result, melatonin levels in the blood rise sharply and you begin to feel less alert. To take advantage of this hormonal phenomenon, you can purchase melatonin over the counter in the United States and Canada and with a prescription in Europe.

Your medical kit

It is a good idea to have a few items in case of emergency. You don't need to stock up to the point of being a mobile medical unit. Many of the medical supplies you can get when you need them at local pharmacies, but if you are going to be traveling far from civilization (for example, if you are crossing the Sahara Desert on camelback, climbing Kilimanjaro, or kayaking down the Amazon), be sure to bring everything you will need for any emergency.

The following are suggestions only. You should design your own medical kit to suit your own situation.

- » Antibiotic ointment (such as Neosporin)
- » Antibiotics (if you are going to be traveling in the outback)
- » Adhesive tape
- » Antibiotic eye drops (for conjunctivitis)
- » Aspirin and minor pain killers
- » Acetaminophen and nasal spray for colds
- » Bactrim or Septra (for internal infections)

» Band Aids (in a roll so you can cut off the size you need)
» 2 or 3 gauze bandages
» Foot powder for long hikes
» Imodium for diarrhea (or other diarrhea pills)
» Lotion for sunburns and dry skin
» Lip salve
» Malaria pills (for the tropics)
» Scopolamine patches and Dramamine tablets (for motion sickness)
» Sleeping pills (melatonin and something heavier like Ambien, which is known by its generic name Zolpidem)
» Sunscreen
» Tiger balm (for headaches and mosquito bites)
» Vitamin E and aloe vera for sunburns
» Any medicines your doctor may prescribe

Travel insurance

My father was recently on a round-the-world cruise on a small ship when he had a heart attack at Santa Maria de Montserrat—a Benedictine abbey located in the mountains near Barcelona. He had to be airlifted to a hospital in the city and undergo a few weeks of treatment. Fortunately, he had purchased the extra travel insurance that encompassed health coverage, flight cancellation, lost luggage, medical coverage on foreign soil, and medical evacuation to your homeland if necessary. In my dad's case, the only thing it did not cover was my stepmother's hotel, taxi, and food expenses. It completely covered his medical expenses and trip back to the United States for both of them. All in all, a $6,000 initial investment in the extra insurance for the year saved them

$500,000 or more, considering they were returned to the United States on private Learjet in the company of both a doctor and a nurse.

———

Travel insurance is a very good idea. Before leaving, research your current insurance coverage to determine whether you are covered abroad. Most travel agencies can arrange a travel insurance policy that includes health and theft coverage. These are good policies to get if you are carrying a camera. One stolen camera can cover the cost of the policy. If you have expensive camera equipment, do not neglect getting insurance.

It is difficult to get insurance for more than a year, so if you are gone for longer than that, you will either have to get someone back home to extend it for you, or you will have to buy a new policy while abroad. A company called World Nomads (worldnomads. com) allows you to buy more coverage online to keep you on the road. They have a multilingual assistance team to help you in more than 150 countries in an emergency, connecting you with medical treatment and transportation.

Many health insurance policies will cover you abroad, but sometimes only in certain countries so be sure to research the facts beforehand. Most health insurance policies require that you first pay the bill and then later get reimbursed.

Some travel insurance packages will also advance you emergency cash if you are in immediate need due to accident, illness, or just bad luck. Falling seriously ill while abroad can be very expensive. If you have to fly back for treatment, the cost can run into the tens of thousands of dollars without insurance.

Recommended reading and websites

The following booklets and publications offer good medical advice for the international traveler.

» Answers.worldnomads.com is a fantastic website with a bulletin board with 89,000 travelers from 129 countries where you can ask almost any question about travel.
» wwwnc.cdc.gov/travel: The U.S. Center for Disease Control and Prevention.
» www.who.int/ith/en/: International travel and health of the World Health Organization (WHO)

18:

Combining Work with Travel

"The world is his,
who has money to go over it."
— *Ralph Waldo Emerson*

In southern France, you can pick grapes in the fall—with decent pay and plenty of good wine.

My first job abroad was at a campground in Germany. I had been traveling for only about six months and still had some savings, but wanted to supplement them while experiencing a new culture. I got the job through a serendipitous family encounter—the daughter of the campground owner had been traveling in Canada and stayed with my mother over the summer before. When I contacted him in Germany he was more than happy to give me a job as a handyman. The experience enabled me to save some deutschmarks (this was prior to the introduction of the euro), while learning the German language and acquainting myself with German beer.

Finding a job

In this chapter I look at finding work while on the road for an extended period, finding ways to volunteer and contribute to the communities you wish to visit and avenues to explore when considering an international career in the private sector, non-profit or official government sectors such as the United Nations.

Unless you are independently wealthy or are traveling for a relatively short period of time, you could run out of money on your travels and need to earn more. You also may want to travel somewhere specifically to work for the summer. Working and living in a country is not only a good way to earn the means to continue traveling, it is a great way to get acquainted with the culture and spend some time to learn the rhythms of the land.

Getting a job abroad is not as easy as it may sound. You will either have to work legally or illegally. "Under the table" work usually entails manual labor, short term, and low pay.

If you are a student, it is easiest to obtain summer employment through any of a number of organizations and institutions that are established for that purpose. The Council on International Educational Exchange (www.ciee.org) operates a unique student work program that cuts through the red tape and arranges for students to get work permits in Britain, Canada, Costa Rica, Czechoslovakia, France, Germany, Jamaica, Ireland, Spain, and New Zealand. CIEE provides its participants with the documentation to work in the country of their choice, along with a list of employers to contact, tips on working in that country, and advice on housing and travel.

The short term and finding work in desperation

In Greece, you can find jobs picking fruit or working on a fishing boat. In southern France, you can pick grapes in the fall—with decent pay and plenty of good wine. Authorities usually turn a blind eye to this kind of temporary work because many locals do not care for hard manual labor. But if you are in it for the experience and to earn some pocket change, working at one of these jobs can be a great diversion from your travels.

Ask at youth hostels and hotels for temporary work. Inquire at your embassy or consulate. While they don't usually offer this service, they may ask around for you if they know you are desperate.

As a last resort, if you are completely out of money, they will send you home on a one-way ticket. When they do this, they will take your passport until you pay the government back and the flight they put you on will probably be expensive.

Sometimes something more stable will present itself if you look hard enough. I found work in Khartoum, Sudan, teaching English to Ethiopian refugees who were being resettled in the United States. I then picked up a gig teaching private English lessons at the American Cultural Center and then in the evenings was hired by a Japanese businessman to teach him English.

In Zanzibar, I found a job teaching English to staff from the Japan International Cooperation Agency (JICA), which provides technical cooperation and other forms of aid promoting economic and social development. In Germany, I worked in a tourist campground. The possibilities are endless, limited only by your imagination and effort.

While traveling in developing countries, visit the offices of international organizations and ask if they, or anyone they know, have work for you. Post notices up at the international clubs. Get someone to invite you into these clubs and then network. Don't leave a single rock unturned.

If you have any skills that may be marketable abroad, bring documentation and letters of reference. If you are a writer, bring clips and a resumé. Don't forget your business cards.

Entertaining and art

If you have any skills at entertaining, be it playing the guitar, painting a picture, or juggling, you probably can earn a decent income in many parts of the world where passersby may have some pocket change to contribute. Even if you only play an instrument amateurishly, you will get a lot of practice on the sidewalk, and soon the coins will start falling from the sky. Additionally, it is a great way to meet people, and enjoy the outdoors. For best results, begin with a few coins in the hat (nobody wants to be the first to give).

Europe is the best place to do this though I know people who have made good money doing it in Japan and Hong Kong as well. It may not work so well in India.

Make jewelry and sell it on the street or in a park. If you have any artistic abilities, get some colored chalk and create a Mona Lisa on the sidewalk. Other artistic skills that can be used to earn quick cash are miming, dancing, or reading tarot cards. Be creative; try something new. The worst thing that can happen is you'll have fun.

Au pair

If you enjoy being with kids, you may consider a job as an au pair. While this is essentially nothing more than a live-in baby sitter, it is a good way to get to know the local culture and language. You work about five hours a day, six days a week, and do everything from watching the children to helping the mother cook and do laundry. InterExchange has been matching au pairs with families for more than twenty-five years. They specialize in placing au pairs with families in the United States, Australia, France, the Netherlands, New Zealand, and Spain. You can reach them at www.interexchange.org.

Traveling with a purpose

More and more people are heading abroad for reasons I call *traveling with a purpose* and to contribute in some way to making the world a better place. There are easy ways to do this, and most involve volunteering in some way. There are some organizations that are there to make this easy for you, from church groups to various branches of the armed forces to government-sponsored volunteer initiatives like the Peace Corps in the United States, or the Volunteer Service Organization (VSO) in Britain.

Volunteering

Working as a volunteer can be a very rewarding and educational experience. It can involve anything from working in a kibbutz in Israel to joining an archaeological dig in Central America.

Most volunteer opportunities involve community service projects that fill certain needs like health care, education, technical

Working as a volunteer can be a very rewarding and educational experience.

consulting, and environmental conservation, such as building a hospital in Africa or restoring a castle in Spain.

Volunteering offers the chance to help a community or contribute to conservation, and it adds value to your resumé. Before signing up for a specific project, potential volunteers should ask where their money is going (placements can be costly) and how past volunteers have made a difference.

International Volunteer HQ, or IVH, claims to be the world's leading volunteer travel company, working in over forty destinations around the world and placing thousands of volunteers abroad every year. IVH provides affordable volunteer programs by partnering with organizations based in each of their program countries. These local organizations are in the best position to see where volunteers are genuinely needed. Whether you want to volunteer and

United Nations Volunteers has mobilized more than 7,000 volunteers who are deployed worldwide.

teach abroad, support wildlife conservation or marine conservation, participate in construction volunteer work, or provide support to staff within childcare centers, IVHQ has volunteer opportunities to suit all motivations and skill sets. If you're pursuing a career in medicine or nursing or if you're a qualified healthcare professional, there are a wide range of medical volunteer abroad opportunities to suit all levels of experience and specialties. A full list of available volunteer projects is available on their website at www.volunteerhq.org.

Blue Ventures develops transformative approaches for catalyzing and sustaining locally led marine conservation. They work in places where the ocean is vital to local cultures and economies and are committed to protecting marine biodiversity in ways that benefit coastal people. Blue Ventures' volunteers learn the diving and scientific skills necessary to collect data that is vital to the management of some of the world's most remote marine biodiversity hotspots. You can apply for one of their opportunities at blueventures.org

United Nations Volunteers (UNV) has mobilized more than 7,000 volunteers who are deployed worldwide. Headquartered in Bonn, Germany, UNV also has an office in New York, four Regional Offices in Bangkok, Dakar, Nairobi, and Panama City that develop regional interventions to advance peace and development, and around eighty field units that represent the organization at the country level. The first step to volunteer abroad with the UN is to determine whether you meet the minimum requirements (visit their website at unv.org). If you qualify, register your profile in their global talent pool. Profiles from the talent pool are then matched with assignments offered by UN partner agencies. Approximately 2,000 assignments become available per year.

Volunteer Forever claims to be a one-stop shop for volunteering abroad. Using their database of 800 international volunteer organizations, 3,500 program reviews, and 11,600 volunteer abroad fundraisers who have collectively raised $2,000,000 for their trips, Volunteer Forever has crunched the numbers to identify a number of top volunteer abroad opportunities. You can explore available opportunities at www.volunteerforever.com.

Volunteer Opportunities You'll Dig

Some archeological projects accept volunteers with little to no archeological training. If you've ever wanted to dig into this field, grab a shovel and contact The Archeological Institute of America. They publish the annual Archeological Fieldwork Opportunities Bulletin, which tells you everything you need to know about getting on current digs around the world. They offer a database of opportunities with the caveat that they don't sponsor excavations and that inclusion in the database doesn't mean that the institute sponsors or endorses any project that's listed as well as the accuracy of any information. That said, you can access their database at www.archaeological.org.

Kibbutzim

My second work experience was unpaid, but all room and board was provided. It was in a kibbutz, which is a type of "commune" unique to Israel. A collective community, traditionally based on agriculture, the first kibbutz was founded by pioneers in 1910. Today, there are more than 270 kibbutzim in Israel and they have diversified greatly since their agricultural beginnings—with many now being privatized. Regardless of their status, the kibbutz offers a unique insight into Israeli society, and are fascinating places in which to live for a while. A kibbutz volunteer is a guest of the kibbutz. It is kind of like visiting friends in a remote location for a few days or weeks and helping them plant or harvest their gardens, wash the dishes, or paint the fences. You wouldn't expect a wage and your friends would take care of all your basic needs.

To be a volunteer at a kibbutz, you do not have to be Jewish. In fact, most volunteers are not. When I arrived at my kibbutz all bright eyed and bushy-tailed in the north of Israel near the border with Lebanon, I had visions of picking fruit under the clear blue sky. Instead, I was put on dish duty in the cafeteria and shortly thereafter was promoted to laundry. By the end of each day I was exhausted. My traveling companion—a Jewish woman from Montreal I met in Jerusalem a few weeks earlier—was far luckier: she picked oranges all day.

If you are interested, get more information at www.kibbutzvolunteer.com/.

Teaching

My third overseas work experience was as a teacher in the Sudan. I arrived in the North African country on a small boat that had traveled the length of Lake Nasser from the dam at Aswan. At Wadi Halfa, I climbed up on the roof of an old train and crossed the Nubian Desert with a small group of roughneck Nubians, arriving in the Sudanese capital of Khartoum a couple of days later with a generous portion of the desert coating my beard and eyelids.

I chose to ride on the roof because I was correctly informed by my nomadic companions that the ticket collectors did not venture up there. In other words, roof travel was free travel.

When I arrived in Khartoum I only had a few hundred dollars left in my money belt. I knew that this would only take me a few more months at best so I found a job with the International Catholic Migration Commission teaching English to Ethiopian refugees who had been accepted into a resettlement program. After three months of English lessons combined with classes on "American orientation," the Ethiopians were flown to host families across the United States.

Teaching English is how most English speakers support themselves during extended stays overseas. Opportunities for this are endless as people in many parts of the world develop a need or desire to learn English. You may find a job teaching English in an American school abroad or in a private language school. Many foreign universities recruit English teachers. In Japan, corporations hire instructors to teach their employees English. Not long after starting my new job teaching English to refugees, a Japanese diplomat from the embassy hired me to give him private lessons in the evenings. Then, on the weekends, I taught English at the American Cultural Centre. A month earlier I was Lawrence of Arabia wearing a turban and surrounded by Nubian Nomads and now I was a clean-shaven English teacher with three jobs.

In six short months, I saved up enough money to continue traveling for another three years. But of more value to me than the money were the experiences and the opportunities to meet some amazing people from Eritrea who were resettled in Arizona. I am still in contact with them more than thirty years later.

Private tutors are in demand in most affluent Asian countries. In South Korea and Taiwan, you may be approached in the street and offered a job. As Asia gears up for more and more trade with the United States, its citizens are finding it good business sense to speak English.

It is usually possible to secure a job overseas teaching English before you even leave home. Check with your local university's career development office or look in the Sunday edition of a large American city newspaper. These positions usually require you to have a university degree (it doesn't matter in what). Most of the job opportunities are in Japan. If you are hired from home, they sometimes will pay for your transportation and always arrange for all your documentation and work permits to be in order.

If you want to find work teaching English in a country after your arrival, you will have to rely a bit on luck and a lot on footwork. Most of the work you will find on your own will be tutoring private individuals, which can be more profitable than working for a university or company, but less secure. Many people who hire you this way will not require a teaching certificate or degree and probably won't ask to see your work permit.

Travelers with a degree in Teaching English as a Foreign Language have the best chance of finding work everywhere. If you have a degree in this field, an organization called the TESOL International Association, formerly Teachers of English to Speakers of Other Languages, is the largest professional organization for teachers of English as a second or foreign language. As of 2013, it had 12,100

Travelers with a degree in Teaching English as a Foreign Language have the best chance of finding work everywhere.

members worldwide and was affiliated with 109 language education organizations, just over half of which were based outside the
United States. TESOL's total number of members, including those
of affiliate organizations, was around 44,000. If you get certified
through them and join their organization, you can receive their period mailings with announcements looking for teachers. For more
information, visit www.tesol.org.

WorldTeach offers highly motivated individuals the opportunity to teach, learn, and grow professionally in developing communities around the globe. They seek inquisitive global citizens
who yearn to do more than simply tour a different country, those
who seek to immerse themselves within a culture, and those who
want to live purposeful lives. With over thirty years of experience
partnering with foreign governments, institutions, organizations,
as well as prestigious universities, they offer their participants un-
paralleled opportunity for personal and professional growth while
bridging world cultures. For more information, visit www.world-
teach.org.

Official volunteer initiatives

The Peace Corps is a U.S. government agency that places both gen-
eralists and specialists into volunteer positions around the world.
Pay is minimal, but you are given a stipend to live on. The Peace
Corps has good cultural and language training programs to prepare
you for your stay, which is usually contracted to a minimum of
two years. Many people use the Peace Corps as a launching pad to
successful international careers with other organizations. The Peace
Corps requires that you either have a four-year degree, or five years
of experience in your field. To sign up, visit www.peacecorps.gov.

Most developed countries have their equivalent of the Peace Corps. In Canada, Cuso International is a development organization that works to reduce poverty and inequality through the efforts of highly skilled volunteers, collaborative partnerships, and compassionate donors. Connect with them at cusointernational.org.

Danish Volunteers (danishvolunteers.com) organize volunteering opportunities, Spanish education, and private accommodations in Guatemala and Nicaragua.

Japan Overseas Cooperation Volunteers (JOCV) dispatches Japanese volunteers overseas and is operated by the Japan International Cooperation Agency (JICA).

Pursuing an international career abroad

The best chances for securing an international career are often found right in your home country and should probably begin with some solid graduate degrees in relevant fields, followed by internships, and then volunteer work with nonprofit organizations to gain experience.

The advice that I usually give to graduate students who are interested in an international career is to go online and find their dream job at the organization of their choice or one as close as possible to what they would ideally like to do. Then take the vacancy announcement, frame it, and turn it into a "to-do list." If the job requires ten years of experience, find a creative way to get that experience—possibly through volunteering for a year then taking a job at a local NGO or start up. If the vacancy announcement asks for fluency in a particular language, then get busy learning that language. (The UN has six official languages and mastering fluency in a few of them will increase your likelihood of getting hired there on top of, of course, degrees and experience in certain technical fields.)

Consider an international MBA, either full-fledged or executive. I did one in two years (TRIUM –accredited through three different universities: Stern at New York University, the London School of Economics, and HEC School of Management in Paris). While the degree doesn't necessarily guarantee success in your job search, it does greatly increase the chances.

Successful long-term international career opportunities are developed through contacts and networking. There is an international corps of expatriates who keep in touch with each other and are constantly meeting in different places. These are the right people to know if you want to work abroad. In today's highly networked world through social media, try and cultivate as many contacts as you can and then nourish them slowly—let them grow. Do not immediately pounce and ask for work but rather build up your experience slowly and prove your value-added net worth in a specific area that is in demand by international organizations.

The following are a few websites that may help in your search for international jobs:

» UNJobs.org has listings from all UN agencies, funds, and programs as well as other international organizations around the world. You can search by job sectors or go search on duty station to see what is available in your preferred location.
» Devex claims to be the media platform for the global development community. It is also a social enterprise working to make the $200 billion aid and development industries do more good for more people and is currently the largest provider of recruiting and business development services for global development.

You can register on their site, access their services, and broadcast your CV at devex.com.

» LinkedIn.com is a must for every job seeker and student. At the very least you should maintain your profile and be as active as possible in the forums as most companies and organizations will look at your profile there when considering hiring you. Ninety-two percent of recruiters use social media in their work today and LinkedIn is the social network they use most. But it is not just a social platform; it has a deep database of opportunities where you can narrow job searches down to sectors and/or locations. If you are not on LinkedIn already, you should be asking yourself why not. If you are in active search mode, pay extra to elevate your exposure.

19:

Studying Abroad

"...there is nothing so far removed from us as to be beyond our reach, or so hidden that we cannot discover it..."

— *René Descartes*

Studying abroad is an excellent way of combining an education with the overseas experience.

There is no better way of experiencing a foreign culture than to live among its people and study with its students. Studying abroad is an excellent way of combining an education with the overseas experience. In fact, more than 60,000 American undergraduate college students are now traveling abroad to study.

There are many types of programs available. You can get involved with an exchange program, participate in a study-abroad program of a U.S. institution, or directly enroll in a foreign university or private school.

If you choose to enroll directly in a foreign university, be sure that you have a firm grasp of the language of study—although many universities abroad do offer English-based programs, such as the Graduate Institute of Geneva, Maastricht University in the Netherlands, or the Asian Institute of Technology in Thailand (to name but a few examples).

Because of the differences between systems of higher education between countries, credits you earn while abroad may not be transferable to your own university. This is okay if you are enrolled in the School of Life and are just there for the learning experience. Otherwise, find out before you get started so you'll know what to expect.

Many universities around the world offer programs specifically for foreigners who want to learn something about the host culture, language, and history. Many of these programs are offered in the summer, but a few are given during the regular semester months. Your classmates will most likely be students from all over the world. Most universities have a foreign studies office with information on opportunities offered by institutions abroad. Or, you can write a consulate of a place you would like to study in and inquire about universities with programs.

Many U.S. universities have programs abroad where you can study language, history, art, folklore, and other subjects. There are also many U.S. organizations that offer opportunities to study abroad. The Council on International Educational Exchange has many programs where you can directly enroll in college and university classes all over the world. CIEE operates more than 175 study abroad programs in more than forty countries and teaching programs in Chile, China,

Most countries have private language schools for both foreigners and locals who want to study foreign languages.

Spain, and Thailand. Summer seminars in twenty-nine countries are available. As the largest sponsor of J-1 visa programs, CIEE organizes seasonal work experiences in the United States for approximately 45,000 university students each year through its Work & Travel USA program. It also organizes high school exchange programs for students in the United States as well as more than thirty countries around the world. Connect with them through ciee.org.

Lastly, there are a few American educational institutions abroad like the American University in Cairo and Sophia University in Japan. It is possible to enroll for a year or more at these schools and transfer the credits directly to your university. Find out more about them by visiting the foreign studies office of your local university.

How much will it cost?

Studying abroad is, surprisingly, not much more expensive than studying in the United States and can actually be cheaper if you choose to study in a country where the dollar is strong or where education is subsidized. Occasionally, if you are on a scholarship at your home institution, arrangements can be made to go to school abroad on your home scholarship.

If you are already in school, you are probably aware of the number of grants, loans, and scholarships that are available. A good information source for available financial aid and how to apply for it can be found at NAFSA: Association of International Educators, which calls itself the world's largest nonprofit association dedicated to international education and exchange that, according to their website, is "working to advance policies and practices that ensure a more interconnected, peaceful world today and for generations to come." You can get more information about their services at nafsa.org.

For an international directory of scholarships in more than 100 countries, get a copy of *Study Abroad* from UNESCO. This useful guide to higher-education study opportunities and scholarships offered by higher education institutions and international organizations in 129 countries presently includes 2,659 entries on courses and scholarships in different higher-education academic and professional disciplines. Included are addresses (including internet sites), admission requirements, application deadlines, financial aid, fees, and living expenses in each country, and other relevant information. Entries are presented in English, French, or Spanish according to the language of the country concerned. Get more information by searching for "UNESCO" and "study abroad" or go directly to www.unesco.org/education/studyingabroad/networking/study-abroad.shtml.

The nontraditional approach

There are several other alternatives available. These options do not earn you credit that you can use toward a degree at an academic institution, but they are a good way to get a memorable educational experience and further you along in the School of Life.

If you will be in a community abroad for any length of time, visit a local school and make friends with the students and teachers. Once you understand the language well enough to communicate, ask if you can sit in on some classes. This type of informal auditing will offer a good learning experience and introduce you to different approaches to education in different parts of the world. You may even offer to teach or tutor English in exchange for being allowed to take classes.

Most countries have private language schools for both foreigners and locals who want to study foreign languages. Offer to teach a class in English in exchange for taking a class in a language of your choice. If you are in Bonn, Germany, you may want to teach English at a private school that also teaches Russian. This way you'll give all three languages a work out!

Another option is self-study. If you are just interested in something, like Egyptology, and want to learn more, travel to Cairo and rent an apartment. Spend time at the museum, the numerous libraries and the universities.

Most cities around the world have excellent libraries where you can do research. If you are a graduate student and are working on a thesis or dissertation, travel abroad to do your research. Besides local libraries, most foreign cultural centers like the British Council or the American Cultural Center have libraries where you can get books on just about any subject. Local universities will not turn you away if you would like to use their libraries. You probably will just have to show your student ID from home. It would also probably help if you had your professor or dean send a letter to the dean of the school in the country where you are interested in doing research.

20:

The Return to "Reality"

"Here I am, safely returned over those peaks from a journey far more beautiful and strange than anything I had hoped for or imagined — how is it that this safe return brings such regret?"

— *Peter Matthiessen*

Traveling is adventurous, but you don't have to be particularly adventurous to travel.

Returning from your travels will, in many ways, be more interesting than your departure. This was especially true for my first big experience abroad. One would think the most severe culture shock happens when you go abroad for the first time, but the opposite can be true for many people. Reverse culture shock is a phenomenon that catches many travelers by surprise. When you get home, you may expect things to be the same, familiar, and comfortable. They will be the same, but the way you perceive them will be different.

Upon your return, you will be a different person, profoundly affected by your travels in ways that will gradually reveal themselves to you for a long time to come. The streets will look different when you return, as will the buildings and the people. The challenging part is that your friends and family may continue to relate to you as the same person, unaware of the changes you have gone through. On the outside, you may look the same, but on the inside, your horizons will have grown beyond anyone's recognition besides yourself.

You will no doubt be excited about your travels and will want to shout about your experiences from the rooftops. Most people will listen for a while, especially family, but somehow they may all seem a bit distant. The problem is that they cannot relate to the places you are talking about and may feel uncomfortable about not being able to understand your passion in the conversation. They will listen with apparent interest as you talk about taking a rickshaw through the streets of Varanasi, but when you stop for a breath, they may interrupt and ask if you missed anything while you were gone.

If you miss talking about other countries and cultures, visit your local youth hostel and make friends with some travelers who are passing through. Remember how you felt when you were alone in a big new city? If you attend a college or university, go to the international association meetings. This will give you a chance to practice your newly acquired language skills.

Sharing what you have learned

While abroad, you will have learned many things that people in your country can only experience through textbooks and television. A good place to share your new insights is at elementary schools. Since we have not inherited the earth from our parents, but are borrowing it from our children, visiting schools is a good way to help prepare the stewards of tomorrow.

Put a slideshow together and talk about the unity of humanity, about the unique beauty of different cultures, and about your adventures. I did this for a few years around parts of Canada and the United States after I returned from my first long journey.

The point is to use what you've learned. Keep in touch with people you met on the road, both fellow travelers and your hosts. You are a traveler now; part of a special family with a kinship that can only be fully appreciated by other travelers.

Most travelers begin planning their next trip right away. Curing itchy feet by traveling is like walking in a bed of poison ivy: The more you walk the itchier they get. You will want to see and experience more and more, acquiring an insatiable appetite for the new and the exciting. The great thing about this world we live in is that it is so full of wonderful things to see and experience that one could be kept busy experiencing more and more for all of one's life. Even if you manage to visit every country in the world, by the time you are done, things will have changed so much in the first country you visited that you could easily start all over.

Mixing work with pleasure

A problem arises when you want to establish a career and be a global vagabond at the same time. This usually limits you to an international field where you can both travel and work. If you don't already have a college degree, this may be the time to consider a career with a global orientation.

As the world gets smaller through increased communication, international business, and transportation, there is a growing need for educated professionals who are familiar with different cultures, traditions, international politics, and languages.

Nearly every imaginable field will have a demand for someone with your people skills and experience, depending on your interests. The foreign services of national governments regularly hire individuals to fill diplomatic and consular positions abroad. International organizations, both governmental and nongovernmental, always need field personnel they can rely on. Most church groups have programs in different countries.

International schools hire people who are familiar with the host culture and give them an edge over other applicants. International expeditions and groups that organize trips often need tour guides who are familiar with local culture, history, language, and folklore of the places they visit. The possibilities are endless.

Bon voyage!

No two travel experiences are alike. What you choose to do and where you plan to go will depend on your own individual likes and dislikes, interests, and ambitions. Traveling is adventurous, but you don't have to be particularly adventurous to travel. You don't have to climb to the highest point in Africa or kayak down the Nile or the Amazon to be considered a traveler. As Robert Louis Stevenson wrote as he was exploring the world at the end of the 19th century: "For my part, I travel not to go anywhere, but to go. I travel for travel's sake. The great affair is to move."

Take Stevenson's advice and step out of your immediate surroundings for a month or a year, and see, hear, feel, and taste how other people live in other parts of your own country and around the world.

While you are there, meet the people. Visit the tourist attractions. See the pyramids, the Taj Mahal, and the Eiffel Tower, but take the time to talk to the people who built them. Whether you are going to Australia, Africa, or Alaska, the efforts you take to learn from your travels will yield numerous rewards for the rest of your life.

About the author

Like the title of this book, Adam Rogers is himself an intrepid traveler. His journeys have taken him to more than 100 countries throughout Europe, Asia, Africa, and the Americas. He set off on his first expedition in his early teens, exploring the west coast of North America from Alaska to Mexico on a motorcycle. At the age of eighteen he left his home in the Yukon Territory with a backpack and an intention to explore the world—to keep traveling east until he ended up back in the west. This first exploration of the planet brought him to more than fifty countries over five years on a budget of less than $100 a month. That experience formed the basis for the first two editions of *The Intrepid Traveler*.

As the editor-in-chief of Los Angeles-based *Earth News*, Adam covered the landmark 1992 Earth Summit in Rio de Janeiro and most of the subsequent summits of the 1990s in Barbados (small island developing states), Cairo (population), Istanbul (cities), Copenhagen (social development), and Beijing (empowerment of women). His book, *The Earth Summit, a Planetary Reckoning*, documented the 1992 conference through the perspectives of youth, business, government, and civil society. Based on that experience, Adam wrote a book for the UN Environment Programme, localizing the framework of Agenda 21 (*Taking Action: An Environmental Guide for You and Your Community*). He also joined a Venezuela/Vermont-based NGO called the Together Foundation to build a global computer-based network (TogetherNet) linking environmental organizations and UN offices around the world to share information

and knowledge – before the worldwide web was invented. Not long after that Adam was involved in an e-commerce start-up (Inter-World Corporation) that pioneered server-side internet archetecture solutions and sold them to Fortune 500 companies like Disney and Marks & Spencer.

Adam left the private sector in 1996 to work full-time for the United Nations, in various positions that lasted twenty-two years, including as coordinator of the World Alliance of Cities Against Poverty – a network of more than 900 cities that are committed to the cause of advancing human development within the urban context. During this time, he also served as a communications advisor to the UN Capital Development Fund (UNCDF), the UN Development Programme (UNDP) and the UN Office for South-South Cooperation (UNOSSC).

Adam received an BA in International Affairs from Northern Arizona University, an MA in Communication and Technology from the University of Alberta in Canada, and an MBA from the TRIUM program at New York University, the London School of Economics, and HEC Paris School of Management. Adam can be reached on twitter at @adamrogers2030.

Appendix: Photography descriptions and credits

Cover: Kyle Cottrell, Unsplash

Title verso: A short stop on the road to Timbuktu, Mali (Adam Rogers).

xiv: A woman smiles in Niger (Adam Rogers).

11:   A child sits contemplatively near a well in Gondar, Ethiopia (Adam Rogers)

12:   Photo of Sebastian Copeland (Keith Heger)

15:   A traveler in Thailand (Shutterstock).

16:   Descending the steps from a temple in Kyoyo, Japan (Adam Rogers)

18:   Selfie on the top of the Cheops pyramid, Egypt (Adam Rogers)

26:   Mismatched shoes in Senegal (Adam Rogers)

36:   Selling sodas on the street in Antigua, Guatemala (Adam Rogers)

38:   A coastal road in Albania (Adam Rogers)

40:   Simonopetra Monastery in Mt. Athos, Greece (Adam Rogers)

45:   A church in Seyðisfjörður, Iceland (Adam Rogers)

48:   A monk at a monastery in northern Thailand (Adam Rogers)

52:   A priest at an Orthodox Church in Gondar, Ethiopia (Adam Rogers)

54:   Woman trying to converse with man in a foreign language (Eldar Nurkovic / Shutterstock).

230:   A market vender in Benin City, Nigeria (Adam Rogers).

234:   Checking email on the go (Yiu Cheung / Shutterstock).

236:   Sending email from rural Vietnam (Adam Rogers).

240:   Getting cash at a bank (Bunyarit Klinsukhon / Shutterstock).

246:   The chef cooking breakfast at the Hotel 2000 in Kigali, Rwanda (Adam Rogers).

248:   Eating Ethiopian food the proper way (Adam Rogers).

251:   Street food in Bangkok (David Kucera / Shutterstock).

252-253: Eating a prepared meal at the top of the Ngorongoro volcano in Virunga National Park in the Democratic Republic of Congo (Adam Rogers).

260:   Border police (Michael Dechev / Shutterstock).

262:   Immigration stamps (Shutterstock).

270:   Armed protection in the Virunga National Park in the Democratic Republic of the Congo (Adam Rogers).

272:   Armed escort near Goma, Democratic Republic of the Congo (Adam Rogers).

277:   Trying to look confident after having just arrived in Senegal (Adam Rogers).

280:   Playing a form of Turkish mahjong in Cappadocia, Turkey (Adam Rogers).

286:   At immigration upon landing at the Geneva International Airport, Switzerland (Adam Rogers).

288:   Thumbs up in Fouta Djallon, Guinea (Adam Rogers).

290:   Eating well (Foxys Forest Manufacture / Shutterstock).

292:   The results of a healthy lifestyle, climbing the seven peaks of Phoenix, Arizona (Adam Rogers).

296:   A nun harvests organic vegetables at a monastery near Phitsanulok, Thailand (Adam Rogers).

316:   Working with the UN in Haiti (Adam Rogers).

318:   Picking grapes in France (Phovoir / Shutterstock).

323:   Young girls at a village near Gorum-Gorum, Burkina Faso
       (Adam Rogers).
324:   Visiting remote areas of Uganda with the United Nations
       (Adam Rogers).
329:   Teaching a class of students in the Philippines (Andrew
       Repp / Shutterstock).
334:   Studying abroad (Jacob Lund / Shutterstock).
336:   Staying with a family while studying Spanish in Antigua,
       Guatemala (Adam Rogers).
338:   Studying abroad (Jacob Lund / Shutterstock).
342:   Fixing a flat tire on the road from Timbuktu to Gao, Mali
       (Adam Rogers).
344:   Near the summit of Aiguille de Bionnassay, on the Italian-
       French border (Adam Rogers).

Made in the USA
Middletown, DE
13 October 2022